May I Have
Your Attention Please

May I Have
Your Attention Please

by
Mike Collins
and
Sergeant Tim McCarthy

MAY I HAVE YOUR
ATTENTION PLEASE
Wit and Wisdom from
the Notre Dame Pressbox

10 9 8 7 6 5 4 3 2 1

ISBN 978-0-9819605-3-1

Published by
Corby Books
A Division of Corby Publishing

Box 93
Notre Dame, IN 46556
(574)784-3482
corbypublishing.com

Manufactured in the United States of America

Table of Contents

Foreword

ONE OF THE THINGS we enjoy most about broadcasting Notre Dame home football games on NBC is the great respect for tradition. That tradition encompasses not only Irish gridiron success but also the pomp and pageantry that surrounds every home game. The Irish Guard and the Band of the Fighting Irish, the best in the land, are certainly part of that spectacular Notre Dame Stadium atmosphere. So too are the many veteran ushers and their special brand of hospitality. The cheerleaders do their part and it wouldn't be an Irish game without the Leprechaun.

Mike Collins and Tim McCarthy are also part of Notre Dame tradition.

Collins has been the Stadium Announcer since 1982, one of only two P.A. announcers for Notre Dame since 1948. To put that in context, there have been eleven different ND football coaches since 1948.

On NBC, we have called Collins "the gold standard of P.A. announcers." Three years ago, when he was inducted into the Notre Dame Monogram Club, then Athletic Director Kevin White said, "your voice is as much a part of this stadium as the players and coaches and it echoes within these walls."

McCarthy is a retired Indiana State Police Sergeant who has been reading his unique safety announcements at the Stadium since 1960. The band plays the 1812 Overture and then McCarthy silences the crowd with his trademark, "May I have your attention please." What follows is sure to elicit cheers/laughs/groans from the crowd. It is never dull.

Quiet and unassuming, Tim McCarthy has become a Notre Dame legend.

So now you can bring some of that special Notre Dame magic into your living room as Mike Collins and Tim McCarthy combine to relive some of the best safety announcements and share press box stories from their many years at the Stadium.

We know you'll enjoy this wonderful slice of Notre Dame tradition.

Pat Haden
Tom Hammond
NBC Sports

Prologue

I WILL NEVER FORGET the first words Tim McCarthy said to me. "Where is Frank and who are you." That was a little imposing but understandable. Long-time Notre Dame public address announcer Frank Croziar decided to retire just two days before the start of the 1982 season and no one had time to tell Tim he had a new "boss" in the booth. And no one told me it was my responsibility to get Tim ready to make his legendary safety announcements.

Our relationship has come a long way since then and it culminates with this book. I could not have a better or nicer partner.

Tim may be on the microphone for thirty seconds a game but he is the rock star in the announcer's booth at Notre Dame. I cannot tell you how many times I have looked over my shoulder while working and spotted a reporter or cameraman or television crew behind me.

I know right away what their first question will be during the next time out. "When does Tim McCarthy show up?"

Actually Tim shows up somewhere in the middle of the third quarter. He is such a good guy that he spends most of his game day elsewhere so he doesn't become a distraction as I am calling the game.

The idea for this book started because Tim has saved every one of his safety announcements since he started in 1960. Think about that. I was still three years away from becoming a freshman at Notre Dame and the Pittsburgh Pirates had just won the greatest World Series ever played.

So to think this guy I heard inside the stadium from 1963 to 1982 would be my co-author some day would have been preposterous. But we are not only colleagues in the booth and print but friends and mutual admirers.

It will be a joy to share some of our time and memories with Notre Dame people because of this book. I hope God will bless us with enough time to write an epilogue together some day.

Mike Collins
The Voice of
Notre Dame Stadium

PART ONE

by
Mike Collins

*Dedicated to my Domer sons,
Tim and Matthew*

-1-

The First Game

EVERY TIME THE PITTSBURGH STEELERS make the NFL playoffs, stories are written about the amazing continuity the Steelers have with head coaches. And by professional sports standards it is amazing—the Steelers have had three coaches since 1969. Still that pales by comparison to public address announcers at Notre Dame Stadium. There have only been two since 1948 and I remain the new kid in the booth to this day.

My predecessor was Frank Croziar who started in 1948 and never missed a game. Frank was a gem of a man who was known as the Dean of South Bend Sportscasters when radio truly ruled the broadcast sports world.

I took over in 1982 and it was a complete surprise. I was sitting in the newsroom of WNDU-TV when the phone rang on Thursday, September 16th. It was legendary Notre Dame Sports Information Director Roger Valdeserri who as calm as could be asked if I could work the game Saturday. At the time I was already doing the PA

1

for the Notre Dame hockey team and I could not understand why the hockey team was playing a game on a Saturday in September. No, Roger said, I mean the football game. Just two days before the start of the season, Frank Crozier had decided to retire and there was no time for job applications or auditions. All I had to do was say yes and the job was mine, so I said yes.

That is when panic set in. I had never done football PA nor for that matter had I ever done football play by play, not even in high school. While I had been in the Notre Dame press box many times I had no idea where the Public Address announcer worked, who worked with him or how the audio system was set up.

And to make matters worse, do you recall why the game with Michigan on September 18th, 1982 was even bigger than it might have looked on the schedule? It was the first night game at Notre Dame and, as I recall, the first coast to coast network television prime time night game other than a bowl game. Notre Dame brought in portable lights from a company in Iowa to make this happen. The only thing I could think of was I not only had a chance to screw up in front of nearly 60-thousand live fans (including my mother) but I could screw up on television from Maine to California.

I always wanted to be a public address announcer.

Some kids want to grow up and be ball players, or doctors or lawyers or, when the Bishop showed up once a year at my grade school in Pittsburgh, some of them lied and said they wanted to be priests. But I wanted to be a PA announcer from the age of 5. That is when my dad took me to my first baseball game, Pittsburgh Pirates and Brooklyn Dodgers at Forbes Field in Pittsburgh. From the moment I heard the voice of Pirate announcer Art Mckennan coming from the speaker behind me, I thought it was the coolest thing in the world a boy could do when he grew up. As a teenager I used to listen to baseball games at night when numerous 50-thousand watt stations would come in and I would strain to hear the PA announcer in the background. And I would mimic them in the basement or backyard.

So a lack of experience and prime time national television was not going to deter me from doing Notre Dame football. This WAS my dream come true, my voice in one of the hallowed palaces of sports in the USA.

But HOW do I do it? The nuts and bolts of it seemed simple enough. Get the rosters of both Michigan and Notre Dame, try to memorize the numbers and names of the key players and when someone threw the ball, ran with the ball or made a tackle, turn on the microphone and say their names. But how to say their names was my issue, what should my demeanor be? That is when I remembered Art, the Pirates long-time announcer. I had a friend in the Pirates front office that gave me his telephone number and I finally got up the nerve to call my boyhood idol. Art could not have been kinder or more helpful, a true gentleman. He said he always thought of himself as a simple liaison to the fans. They were there to see the ballplayers, not to listen to the PA announcer; that no one was paying a dime of the ticket price to hear me and I doubt, he said, anyone will pay an extra dime on their Notre Dame football ticket applications to hear you. And don't be a cheerleader he told me. Notre Dame has cheerleaders on the field. You have one job to do and that is to keep the fans informed. And he said always be a professional—Notre Dame is a classy place and you should be just as classy.

I have followed Art's advice for all of the years since. I have never once given my name over the public address system and I have done maybe two short interviews about my job.

Art managed to calm my nerves a bit as the hours dwindled to my first game. But as I look back it was comical. For one thing I forgot to get a credential, the only way you can get into the press box. Someone had to go and get Roger Valdeserri to let me in. I also forgot to ask if I was going to get paid, if I had a place to park or where the PA booth actually was.

Somehow, someway, I got through that first game and I thought I did okay. I was so tied up in just trying to do the job without making a big mistake that all of these years later I could not remember who won the game (thank you, google, for telling me Notre Dame beat Michigan 23 to 17) or what network was carrying the national broadcast (CBS). I do recall that a cold beer after the game never tasted so good. And I remember two phone calls I got on Monday. The first was from Roger saying I had passed the test and he was keeping me, in other words, that game was my audition.

The other call was from Art, my boyhood idol. He told me he watched the game with the sound turned up and he thought Notre Dame's new Public Address announcer was a real pro. I may have forgotten many details of that first game but I have never forgotten those phone calls.

-2-

Tuialailefaleula

WHAT WOULD HAPPEN if you used the above word in a game of Scrabble? Let us ponder the possibilities. First you would probably wipe out your remaining letters. You would then become a Scrabble legend in your family and the neighborhood because I am guessing this would lead to international fame since it is unlikely that anyone in the long history of scrabble has ever used that word. You could probably get a reserved seat at the World Series of Scrabble in Las Vegas which, of course, would be televised on ESPN because if people will actually sit in front of a television to watch poker, you would think Scrabble on TV cannot be far behind.

Well you cannot use that word in Scrabble but you could find it in a crossword puzzle. Think of the possibilities of connecting crosswords when you put in one word with 10 vowels. I think I shall inform the *New York Times* of this and then just wait with baited breath until my wife asks me for help some Sunday morning as she always does when there is a clue that has something to do with sports or rock and roll.

The reason you cannot use the word in Scrabble but can use it in a crossword puzzle is that it is a name of a person. Actually it is TUI ALAILEFALEULA. I believe it is a ten-syllable name, which might be some kind of a record. While there are only two fewer letters in my name, sadly I fall six syllables short of Tui.

So the clue in the crossword puzzle would be "offensive lineman for the University of Washington in 2004."

And of course it was just my luck that Washington was on the Fighting Irish home schedule in 2004.

I have a set-in-stone system when preparing to do a game at Notre Dame Stadium. First, I take them one at a time. On the Tuesday before a home game I go to the Sports Information office and pick up all the necessary material, rosters, depth charts, special announcements, etc. Usually I do not go over pronunciations until Friday night because I have a short memory span. For whatever reason I took a peak at the Washington roster on that Tuesday. Now Washington has a long history of recruiting student-athletes from the South Pacific so I was prepared for some shock to the system and there were more than a few tongue twisters; but when I got to Tui Alailefaleula, panic set in. I showed it to my wife who said, as you would expect, how DO you pronounce that? I tried and it was hilarious, as if I had started drinking say around noon. Yes, the Washington media guide had a pronunciation chart but when it comes to ten syllables, that can often make it even more confusing.

Now remember my pal TUI is an offensive lineman and you can go an entire game as PA announcer without naming one offensive lineman unless, of course, he recovers a fumble and I am so paranoid that I convince myself that Washington's quarterback will drop the ball ten times during the game and all ten fumbles will be recovered, miraculously, by TUI.

So I come up with a brilliant idea and track down the Washington play by play announcers in Seattle and give them a call for emergency assistance. They tell me they just call him Tui! Great, just great. If I just call him Tui on one of his ten fumble recoveries someone in the stands will yell at the top of his voice "chicken." Still they help me out enough that when I go back to the pronunciation guide, the name starts to come into focus. And when I am doing my last minute homework Friday night my wife, Melissa, asks, "Honey let me see if you can pronounce the name." I give it a shot as she looks at the roster and she thinks I have it down pat. I do too and I am pretty darn proud of myself.

So now it is game day and I am ready to show off. Washington's Sports Information director, Jim "Spook" Jacobs is a friend of mine from the days when he was an assistant at Notre Dame so you can only imagine how excited I am to preen in front of a friend. So I sit down with Jim to go over his roster, but instead of going over the names from A to Z, I start at the bottom and work my way backwards. The excitement is so palatable my palms are sweating.

Now I get to that name (with a cheat sheet in my shirt pocket) and I NAIL it. Yes!

Whereupon Spook tells me Tui Alailefaleula did not make the trip. Huh? "He's hurt."

How could Tui do this to me? I am thinking maybe I could wish Tui a speedy recovery on behalf of all of his friends at Notre Dame. Of course, I don't so I have to go back an entire decade to recall my greatest hit, Tim Biakabutuka from Michigan.

By the way, I did not catch this until I started writing this piece. Tui Alailefaleula is not from the South Pacific, he is from Anchorage, Alaska.

-3-

My Waterloo

IF THERE IS ANY ONE THING that drives me to do a good
job in the PA booth at Notre Dame Stadium it is fear. Fear
of making a mistake and having 80-thousand in person
human beings howling in laughter at me. Think about
it. If Bruce Springsteen screws up the lyrics to "Born to
Run" in concert the odds are good it will be in front of
fewer than 80-thousand fans.

Now simple mistakes, like mis-identifying a player,
you would think would not cause people to act as if they
are watching Comedy Central. Or make them shout out
at you.

So we have a few rules in place, like no profanity
in the booth at any time. Should a four-letter word leak
through the microphone, I can assure you that would be a
one-way ticket for me to get thrown out of the Stadium.

This has not always been the easiest rule to enforce.
One of my long-time spotters is Brian Boulac, a former
assistant coach, and one of the finest people I have ever
met at Notre Dame. Brian is a great spotter and I cannot tell you how much I rely on him especially when it

appears to me that any one of eight guys could have made a tackle. Somehow Brian always figures out who got there first.

But as I mentioned Brian is a former coach and, so I have been told, coaches occasionally use four-letter words. Well as I found out, once a coach, always a coach. Early on in our first season together, almost always when things were not going well, Brian would utter the occasional four-letter word. This had to stop so I reminded Brian of a few things like Our Lady and the priests in attendance and his wife and children and eternal damnation.

That did it though I must admit hearing a former coach say things like "golly, gee whiz, that sure was a dumb play" just doesn't fit the stereotype.

But mistakes will be made and my biggest or at least most infamous occurred in the mid-80s. We were playing Navy and even though it was early November it was the coldest day ever for me at the Stadium and I have been to every game since 1963. The wind was howling and lake effect snow seemed to be coming down in huge bursts. I found out later the wind chill bottomed out during the game at minus seven. I am sitting on a hard metal stool and the cord to the microphone was not long enough to even stand up. I was frozen in place and all I wanted was for the game to end. Most of the fans took matters into their own hands, or in this case their feet, and left. I have never seen fewer fans in Notre Dame Stadium during the fourth quarter than I did on that day.

You might recall that Navy had a terrific running back during that period by the name of Napoleon McCallum. He was a legitimate All-American candidate and to burnish his credentials and with the Naval Academy trailing badly all they did in the fourth quarter was hand the ball off to McCallum. So with my brain frozen I just kept repeating on Navy's final drive "that's McCallum on the carry for a gain of four" or whatever.

What I did not notice, remember the snow made it hard to see across the field, was that after McCallum was tackled near his own sideline he went to the bench probably to save himself from hypothermia. Navy runs the ball on the next play and like a one trick dog I just repeated myself, "that's McCallum on the carry for a gain of two."

Lo and behold some fan directly below my booth yells at the top of his voice "that was Smith you idiot." So I'm thinking what does this guy care and why is he so dumb that he is still here? Anyway no one I know is still in the stands to hear me being called an idiot so forget about it, its over and I am out of here.

These were still the days when an edited version of Notre Dame games was played on television the next day.

That Sunday I am in my easy chair, still covered in three or four blankets, reading the *South Bend Tribune* with the replay on television. Yep, you guessed right. As clear as a bell after someone other than Napoleon McCallum carried the ball I could hear in the background "that was Smith you idiot." I just stared at the television, practically frozen in place!

-4-

Sorry Mom

THERE IS NO WORK I have done in my life that has been more satisfying than being the public address announcer at Notre Dame Stadium. But it is work and that is the only way I can approach it, as a job. Everything happens fast beginning about ten minutes before kickoff and it stays that way for the next several hours. While some fans are exasperated by the lengthy television timeouts, most of those I have to fill, often with announcements that have been changed on the fly. Just like a player I have to stay focused because any letdown could lead to a mistake and there is NO way I could live with a mistake that takes the fans attention away from the game. In other essays I have mentioned a couple of funny things that have happened over the many years but I am proud that there have only been a couple.

So what keeps me focused is routine, rules and nervousness. Oh if you only knew. I spent nearly all of my career doing somewhere around 23 thousand live local newscasts but those were a walk in the park compared to game day. I try to relieve the pressure by keeping to a routine, a rigid routine. It starts on Tuesday of game week when I pick up all of the game notes and rosters and spend at least two nights going over those names and numbers. On Fridays I begin a military like operation. I pick up all of the game announcements and the timing sheet. You might be surprised at how the athletic department has everything laid out. It is right down to the minute. Friday night I stay at home and go over everything repeatedly and the only time I talk to my wife is to pronounce a players names. By this point I only know the players names, my wife, two dogs and a cat I might be able to recall.

The first home game of the season is the toughest, I really wish the Irish would always open on the road. I do not talk to anyone in the morning except myself. Actually I shout at myself. I go out on our porch, shut the door and start talking VERY loud. The neighbors had to be warned because I did not want to be hauled off for psychological examinations.

There is a reason for this. I am trying to stretch my voice. No one actually talks like a public address announcer except maybe my father when I screwed up as a kid. As the hours count down, the routine gets even more rigid. I MUST leave for the stadium two and a half hours before the game and I don't care who is going with us because, really, they only like to use my nice parking pass anyway.

About four years after I started my mother learned this the hard way. Sadly my dad never could come to a game after I started but mom was always spry and loved nothing more than sitting on a wooden bench with splinters for three and a half hours watching football. She is coming out and knows the two- and- a- half hour rule. There must have been a traffic snarl on the Indiana Toll Road so mom is late. So I left without her. As I pulled away I did check the rearview mirror but still, no mom, so I kept going. Now it is not as bad as you might be thinking. The worst case scenario would have been a mere mile and a half walk. She did get a ride from some Notre Dame friends whom I had informed of her misfortune. I must say she was rather cool towards her son at the post game tailgate party but we did give her a ride home.

Then there was the time in the mid-90's when I left something even more more important behind than my mom. Again this was the first game of the season and I am a wreck. Our friends arrive on time (and they came from St. Louis, unlike mom) and we take off. At the corner of South Bend Avenue and Angela my friend Ralph asks me where my briefcase is. What briefcase? The one with all of your rosters, game notes, announcements and binoculars. I swear to God, I was so nervous I forgot everything? We had to go back and for the first and only time the routine was broken.

The next day I told my mom what happened. "Serves, you right," she said.

-5-

Penn State

IT IS A NATURAL THING to ask and the question has been posed to me dozens of times over the years. What are my most memorable games since I started as public address announcer in 1982? Ironically I do not have a list and the only way I could put one together is to go through each season and start from scratch. In part that is because there are no "big" games or "little" games to me. Each game has to be taken with the same dedication and when one game is over I get it out of my mind and start thinking of the next game.

But I do have memories and one opponent that mean more to me than the others and it is not USC or Michigan, it is Penn State.

In part that is because I was born and raised in Western Pennsylvania and my roots are still there. But, even at that, I grew up a Pitt fan and Pitt and Penn State fans had clear demarcation lines, like somewhere around Altoona. It is a sports tragedy that Joe Paterno ended this great series.

I owe my introduction and lifelong love of college

football to the University of Pittsburgh. Growing up in the 1950s, Pitt football endeared its programs to boys like me. There were all kinds of ways to get in for free, Boy Scouts, Altar Boys, good grades and, as I recall, if you delivered newspapers. Right there that covered you for four games a year, which was all but one on a home schedule back then. If Notre Dame was playing at Pittsburgh in a given season you knew that would not be one of a young boy's freebies, because it was the only guaranteed sellout.

All these years later I remember my dad coming home one day from his job at US Steel with a surprise. It was two tickets to see Notre Dame at Pitt Stadium. For at least two months those tickets were on a table next to my bed and every morning the first thing I did was check to make sure they were still there. Notre Dame! You mean that team I listened to every Saturday on the radio? The team that played somewhere in Indiana and all of the priests and nuns at St. Wendelin's Grade School prayed for secretly or even openly? The team with Paul Horning who was on the cover of all of those magazines I had saved in a box in my room? Yes, that team!

First the months, then the weeks and then days and hours could not pass fast enough. And the only thing I remember about that game today is that it was played in a monsoon and I didn't care because the sun was shining on me. Ironically, the first time I ever saw Notre Dame play in South Bend, it was against Michigan State my senior year in high school and that game was played in a continuous downpour. I had never been west of Cleveland in my life so getting soaked to the bones was not going to challenge me.

So I think the weather has a lot to do with my favorite moments after more than a quarter century in the public address booth. And that means Penn State and Notre Dame. It seems like every time The Nittany Lions played here in the on again, off again series the sun never came out. It was cold and cloudy and often snowing. Could anything be more perfect? Well, yes. The two teams played old fashioned football as if Woody Hayes was coaching both teams. They hit and they hit hard and they got really dirty (as in mud) and they wore uniforms that some people might call bland but I call classics. They also had a lot of big hulking players who looked like the only way they could enjoy these match ups even more is if there were no referees. Just do it toe to toe and the last man standing claims victory for his university.

It was the 1992 game that epitomized this series more than any other. That is the one with the snow flying everywhere. Some of the best college football pictures I have ever seen were taken that day by Michael Bennett who continues today as ND photographer extraodinaire.

You can find them still hanging in bars, restaurants and offices throughout the South Bend area. This is a game that should have been televised in black and white with Lindsay Nelson doing play by play.

It was gut wrenching to watch this one as the teams went back and forth, no one giving ground emotionally. Notre Dame needed every ounce of emotion to pull it out with a last minute drive that ended with a Reggie Brooks touchdown and a Jerome Bettis two-point conversion. Looking back on it, doesn't it seem perfect that Jerome Bettis, my favorite Notre Dame player in all of these years, is the one who beat Penn State?

It sure does to me because the only place in the USA where the cheering might have matched South Bend was Pittsburgh. And somehow I think it was destiny that would lead Jerome Bettis eventually to become the hero of the Pittsburgh Steelers.

Notre Dame and Penn State, now that is what college football should be all about.

-6-

Bush Push

IT WAS A MOMENT in the Public Address booth I will never forget, one of the most famous moments ever at Notre Dame Stadium and I wish that it had never happened.

Maybe it will turn out to be the one game I will remember above all others, which is odd since Notre Dame lost the game. Or should I say Notre Dame won the game, and then lost the game. But, in the end, the only thing that matters is the final score.

It was Notre Dame and USC, October 2005 and the Irish are having a dream season, visions of a return to the top of the college football world are everywhere. The campus was in a frenzy for a week, yes it seemed the like the good old days were back.

USC was back by then, the best program in the country with superstars galore and here they were playing their archrival. You had the feeling this is the way it was going to be for years to come, the Irish and the Trojans will settle the National Championship on the field during the regular season.

I try to take every game with the same dedication and passion and remember all the time to keep my cool. That was easier said than done for me.

All week long I couldn't shake something from the past. My sophomore year at Notre Dame was the beginning of the Era of Ara. It might be nostalgia but for me there has not been a season like that since because, truth be told, no one expected it.

Joe Doyle broke the story of Ara's hiring in the *South Bend Tribune* in December of 1963 and the first we heard of it was seeing the newspaper at the train station as we were heading home for Christmas break.

Let me tell you what the reaction was at the time. First, no one could pronounce Ara's last name. And then there were complaints about hiring a coach from Northwestern, and this is hard to believe today, not hiring a "Notre Dame man." Some people even complained that Ara was not Catholic. Poor Ara. He also inherited a team that won two games in 1963 under interim coach Hughie Devore. A good trivia question about that 1963 season is that Notre Dame's victories came back to back over USC and UCLA, so at least Hughie won California.

Ara's first game was against Wisconsin and we listened to it in our dorms and could hardly believe what was happening, in fact some students just assumed it was a freakish thing and Wisconsin just wasn't very good. But then the victories started piling up and suddenly people knew how to pronounce Ara's last name and could care less if he were Hindu.

Now it was off to Southern California. To this day I remain amazed at the number of people who tell me they watched the game, one of the most exciting games they had ever seen. That is interesting but the game was only televised in Los Angeles and South Bend. WNDU-TV, a station that was way ahead of the times in broadcasting live games, did its own production and direction. The game was played on the Saturday of Thanksgiving weekend and I was one of several hundred students who decided to forgo mom's home cooking and stay on campus to watch the game.

We were in Morrisey Hall, five of us in a room on the first floor with a black and white television with rabbit ears.

We thought we had it won and the National Championship was ours, Notre Dame is back in its rightful place. Then our hearts were broken, USC marched down the field and two names that will live forever in my hall of infamy, Craig Fertig to Rod Sherman stuck a dagger into Irish fans everywhere. Remember if these two villains had not connected like they did, the title was ours because then the final poll came before the bowl games.

We were in a daze and refused to believe what we

had just seen. I swear this is true. Several of us stayed up late to wait for the last South Shore train to arrive in downtown South Bend. We walked to the station to get the first editions of the Chicago newspapers convinced that when they dropped on the platform the outcome of the game would be different but no, we lost in the newspapers too.

All of that was in mind in 2005 but this time around I could not drink a six-pack of beer to drown my sorrow or scream at the television. I had to be cool or at least close to cool. This was unreal. It was 1964 all over again. Notre Dame comes down the field and the gutsy Brady Quinn dives into the end zone to give the Irish the lead. But, just like '64, USC comes back and now it is do or die. And it looked like Notre Dame did! USC quarterback Matt Leinart goes for the winning score but is out of control and loses the ball, it dribbles and bounces and the clock goes down to triple zeroes. There is only one problem—I knew the game was not over. As I was trained to do, the split second the ball crossed the sideline I checked the clock. Then it really got crazy. Fans, not just students, stormed the field. There was not enough time for me to check with game management or security or anyone for that matter. So I hit the button and in the sternest voice possible said, "The game is not over. If you do not leave the field now your team will be penalized." Suddenly, as my wife described it after the game, "it was like the parting of the Red Sea," the crowd on the field turned as one and returned to their seats. We know what happened next: Reggie Bush pushed Leinart into the end zone for the winning touchdown.

I felt terrible. We lost the game and thought I was a jerk for "hollering" at the students. I never wanted to part the Red Sea; I just wanted to pick up the Sunday newspaper and find out that Notre Dame beat USC.

-7-

Joe Sassano

No one has helped me longer or with more dedication in the announcer's booth at the stadium than Joe Sassano. That name is familiar to everyone at Notre Dame and to many beyond campus because of his achievements at the Joyce Center. But before I get to that, this would be a good time to explain the system we use on game day. To the occasional outsider who wanders in it might appear akin to a sophisticated military operation. Actually it is quite simple but rigid. With a few tweaks over the years we now follow the same routine and hard and fast rules from one game to the next, one season to the next.

There are three of us (four counting band announcer Jon Thompson), myself, Brian Boulac and Joe. In addition to doing the play by play, I spot both teams' offenses, Brian spots both teams' defenses and Joe keeps the yards gained, or lost, on every play. He is the only one of the three of us who CAN do that because Brian and myself use binoculars on every play, which means our field of vision is no more than ten yards. Remember we

29

are, in effect, on the fourth level of the stadium. Without the binoculars, a fan sitting on the forty-yard line would have a better view of all the numbers involved in a play.

All of this information is available to us from the main press box and we also have a television monitor in the booth. However, we just cannot wait. We try to get the information out to the fans within two seconds of the conclusion of a play. We only use the television monitor to sort out something that was no clearer to us than it was to the average fan, like the blocker of a kick when there has been a bit of a scrum or when someone might have tipped a ball at the line of scrimmage.

While there is a distinction in duties we also work as a team on every play. I sit in the middle, Brian to my left, Joe to my right. Taking the most simple of plays, a run up the middle, I will call out the name and number and instantly make sure Brian agrees. He then follows by telling me the name and number of the tackler or tacklers and I turn to Joe to give me the gain (or loss) on the play. I swear that all happens in two seconds and then I hit the button, turn on the microphone and make the announcement.

Joe started working with me two years after I started and he came with valuable experience that made my job a lot easier. For six years he did the color commentary alongside Tom Dennin on the WNDU broadcasts of Notre

Dame football. As I mentioned elsewhere, WNDU was a cut above most local television stations. The station produced and broadcast nearly all Notre Dame games that were not picked up by the network with the NCAA contract. Remember this was before cable and at a time when any one school was limited to how many national broadcasts it could be involved in. So that meant WNDU, and veteran producer and director Steve Horvath, did an awful lot of games that only fans in the South Bend market could watch.

Joe then spent another five years (1975 to 1980) as part of the Mutual Radio broadcast crew. So by the time he joined me in 1984, he had the exact experience I needed at my side to make quick accurate calls for the fans.

While I appreciate everything Joe has done for me in the booth, it would be hard to match what he did for me as part of his long-time job at the Joyce Center. As I write this, the Joyce arena is undergoing its first major renovation since it opened more than forty years ago. Joe was there from the beginning as Director of Programming and Special Events.

And what a job he did with that title and it is something that, for many reasons, will never be eclipsed. It was Joe who brought to Notre Dame and the South Bend community an array of major entertainment that easily rivaled much larger markets, which was one of the promises made when money was being raised to build the ACC, much of it from the greater South Bend area. It was a promise kept and then some.

And on January 26th, 1981 Joe did something for me that I remember like it was yesterday. He made it possible for me to not only meet Bruce Springsteen but to spend some quality time with The Boss as well. Though if Joe knew at the time I was hanging out with the talent, he might not have been too pleased.

Here is how it played out. Joe put me on his staff for the day and told the promoters I would be available for any necessary duties that would come up throughout the day and night. He "suggested" that I be assigned to Bruce's dressing room, basically standing outside the door so no one wandered in. Springsteen had one dressing room, the E Street Band another. So there I was when the band came inside the Joyce, first for the warm-ups and then to chill out and put together a set list for the night. Bruce gave me a smile and a handshake before he entered his room. The temptation was too much and what was I going to do with the Notre Dame bookstore bag filled with a hat and sweatshirt for Bruce and album covers all ready to be autographed? So I got up my nerve and knocked on the door. Only two things could happen at this point and one of them would not be good. To my surprise, I was invited in. But, I asked, who is going to guard the door? Lock it, said Springsteen and, by the way, would you like a Heineken? Are you kidding me! So I watched Bruce put together a set list for the night, he asked if I had a request (I did, the classic frat-rock song "Double Shot of My Baby's Love") and then he noticed my stuffed to the gills bookstore bag. He gladly accepted the hat and sweatshirt and not only signed every piece of memorabilia I had, he also took one of the album covers to the other dressing room and had the entire band sign it. By the way, he left the ACC after the show wearing my hat.

So now you understand why I have seen Bruce Springsteen 75 times and I will always owe Joe Sassano big time.

-8-

Notre Dame's Football Historian

IT WOULD BE HARD to imagine any nine year old today doing or even wanting to do what Joe Doyle did when he was nine years old. He worked for a newspaper. He was too young to deliver newspapers so he got a job as a proofreader at the South Wayne *Homestead* in Wisconsin. True story from a guy who has had black and white running through his veins all of his life. By the way, Joe was paid fifty cents a day to do his job which was more than enough to buy all the ice cream a kid could ever want. Today a nine year old might have his or her own Internet blog but a career in newspapers? I don't think so.

All these years later Joe remains a newspaper guy. He still writes a column on football Saturdays for the *South Bend Tribune* and he is the longest serving member of the media in the Notre Dame press box. Oh, and young pups like myself still go to him for advice and a historical perspective.

Joe came to Notre Dame in 1946 (and it was not uncommon then), as a 25 year old after he completed his military service. Notre Dame did not have a newspaper then, in fact Notre Dame did not have a regular news-paper, *The Observer,* until one of my dormmates, Robert Sam Anson, founded it in the mid-60s. So Joe went to work for the *Scholastic Magazine,* which clearly knew talent because they made Joe Doyle editor his senior year. He graduated in January of 1949 and went to work at the *Tribune* a month later. Amazingly, up until then Joe had never covered sports. But he caught a break later that year. Notre Dame was playing at home but the big game of the year was in Ann Arbor, Michigan versus Army. The *Tribune* sent Joe to cover that game, liked what they read, let him cover a few more games in 1950 and made him Sports Editor in 1951. Now that is what I call being on the fast track. Can you even imagine this today, the guy is barely out of college and he is covering the most successful team and most legendary coach, Frank Leahy, in all of college football!

As mentioned in another piece in this book, it was Joe who broke the news that Ara Parseghian was taking over the Notre Dame football program in December of 1963. Try as I might, I could not to this day pin Joe down on how he got the scoop. He and Ara remain the clos-est of friends even now, which, of course, could never happen today. The ground rules for their relationship were set early on when Joe wrote a story that Ara did not particularly like.

The conversation went like this:

Ara: Where did you get that story?

Joe: None of your %#* business. I won't tell you how to coach, so don't tell me how to write a column.

Ara: Okay.

And that sealed the deal and nearly every morning during the Era of Ara, the two of them met for coffee at some ungodly hour and it worked because they had one rule, we don't talk football.

By the way, Joe Doyle did debunk one story that went around for years. Rumor had it that Ara went to the Fathers Hesburgh and Joyce and asked for a one year sabbatical to clear up some health issues and, again according to the rumor, he was turned down. Joe says that is not true. In fact it was Father Joyce who offered the sabbatical to help out Ara but both Ara, and more importantly his wife Katie, did not think that would work. And that was it, the end of the Era of Ara but not the end of a friendship between the two men that continues today.

Journalists are taught to never have favorites so I was a bit reluctant to ask Joe something I was always tempted to ask: What would be your all-time Notre Dame football team?

Guess what? He gave it to me after hours of diligent

digging. The greatest writer to cover the Notre Dame football beat has his all-time team, covering more than a half century.

Feel free to get in touch and argue your point but keep something in mind—Joe Doyle *is* the all time expert.

Joe Doyle's All-Time Notre Dame Team

OFFENSE
First Team

Ends: Leon Hart, Dave Casper
Tackles: George Connor, George Kunz
Guards: Tom Regner, Ray Lemek
Center: George Goeddeke
Quarterback: Tom Clements
Halfbacks: John Lattner, Nick Eddy
Fullback: Jerome Heavens

DEFENSE:
First Team

Ends: Alan Page, Ross Browner
Tackles: Pete Duranko, Mike McCoy
Linebackers: Jim Lynch, Bob Golic, Bob Crable, Bob Olson
Backs: John Lujack, Nick Rassas, Jeff Burris
Specialists: Rocket Ismail, Tim Brown
Punter Craig Hentrich
Place Kicker: Bob Thomas

Second Team

Ends: Tom Gatewood, Tim Brown
Tackles: Bob Kuechenberg, Bob Toneff
Guards: Dick Arrington, Larry DiNardo
Center: Jim Schrader
Quarterback: Joe theismann
Halfbacks: Emil Sitko, Vagas Ferguson
Fullback: Paul Hornung

Second Team:

Ends: Jim Martin, Mike Kadish
Tackles: Bryant Young, Aaron Taylor
Linebackers: Ned Bolcar, Jim O'Malley, Jerry Groom
Backs: Dave Waymer, Bobby Taylor, Allen Rossum, Tom Schoen
Punter: Joe Restic
Place Kicker: John Carney, Dave Reeve

Coach
Ara Parseghian
Best All-Around Player
Paul Hornung

-9-

The Old House

1963 WAS THE END of an era at Notre Dame Stadium though I doubt if even a few of you remember it. That was the last season the freshman class, all stuffed into the north end zone seats, held up a sea of placards to start a cheer. The placards were two sided and when told to do so we were all to hold up side "A" for something like Go Irish and then flip them to side "B" for another not so catchy phrase.

This short-lived tradition came to an end for several reasons. First, the freshmen hated the idea because we might as well have hung big signs around our necks saying "we are freshmen, please abuse us." Second, 1963 was a lousy year for Notre Dame football after several mediocre years, at best; and third, being freshmen, we really enjoyed using the signs as square Frisbees and sailing them as far as we could. With four heavy-duty pointed corners this was not a good idea.

Not only did the sea of placards end in 1963, that was also the last time I ever sat in a seat at Notre Dame

Stadium. From 1964 until today I have always been doing something other than being a fan at Notre Dame home games.

Even during my freshman year I was hanging around the Sports Information Department, which was located in the basement of Breen-Phillips Hall. In fact, the entire Athletic Department was there other than the football coaches who had offices in The Rockne Memorial Building.

I had been befriended by long-time SID Charlie Callahan who, at first, let me organize his files. This was no easy task since Charlie was an Irishman through and through and organization was not one of his many skills.

By the 1964 season Charlie trusted me enough to give me odd jobs in the press box which, up to then, was one of the most exciting sports thrills of my life. Sure, all I was doing was running the mimeograph machine and then passing out statistics quarter by quarter to the media but just to be in the presence of sports writers from around the country was mind boggling. The single strongest remembrance I have from that era is that there was ONE woman in the press box, ONE. She ran the Western Union ticker that sent updated scores around the nation. I believe there was no male capable of doing this.

With each year while a student, Charlie gave me

more and more responsibilities. I kept statistics, was assigned to the coaches' post-game press conference to take down some quotes that then would be assembled, mimeographed and handed out to the media just in case some of them were too lazy to actually write down the quotes themselves. My most important duty, as far as the sportswriters were concerned, came long after the game ended. The writers back then would return to the press box to type their stories and this could take hours after the final gun. It was my "unofficial" responsibility to make sure they did not run out of cigarettes or refreshments, if you know what I mean. Since I was not 21 and did not have a car, Charlie Callahan trusted me enough to give me a key to his secret refreshment cabinet and the press box had a cigarette machine. This was a pretty good deal because even a sportswriter would give you an occasional tip when his supply of cigarettes and his glass were replenished.

When I finished as a student in 1967, it was Charlie who lined up interviews for me that paved the way for my career in broadcasting and so I stayed in South Bend all of my adult life. I also stayed active on football Saturdays somewhere other than the seating area.

That includes ten years as a freelance photographer. I was a pretty good amateur photographer and first Roger Valdiserri (who succeeded Charlie) and later John Heisler worked out a nice arrangement for me. I got a photographers' sideline pass and they got the pictures just in case I captured something the real photographers missed.

So one way or another I worked on those football Saturdays until I got the call in 1982 to be the Public Address announcer.

Amazingly, even by 1982 I had never been inside the public address booth, which then and even today is known as the broadcast booth. To say the least, it was a bit of a surprise. It was cramped, had no heat or air, wires dangled from the ceiling, and there was a series of pipes just above and behind my head. I cannot tell you how many times I stood up at an exciting moment in the game and whacked the back of my head on those pipes. There was one 75-watt light bulb in there and to this day I am thankful that the spotter I inherited, Ted Andrews of the *South Bend Tribune,* knew enough about the dank dark place to bring a flashlight to my first game, which, as mentioned elsewhere, was the first night game at Notre Dame Stadium. Ted held the flashlight over the rosters so I could read them. The walkway to my booth and the radio and television booths was so small that people could not pass one another in it. So, for instance, if I was coming from the north and, say, Paul Hornung was coming from the south, I always backed up to let him pass.

Now I was not expecting a suite or a skybox but this was something else. In fact we did not have chairs but instead hard cold metal stools. I still have mine; Notre Dame gave it to me when the press box and stadium were renovated. Even when I look at it today it reminds me of a stool the police used to use to interrogate a suspect. Though my stool had "PA" stenciled on it and I bet you don't find a lot of those down at the jail.

Still, the place grew on me. I even learned to duck when I stood up and, about ten years into my tour of duty, I was given a space heater.

Truth be told, I fell in love with the place—it really did feel like it was my personal space at Notre Dame. And when the season ended before the renovation began I stayed there for well over an hour and just stared. Thankfully, most of the lights were out by the time I left the stadium because that helped conceal the tears I had in my eyes.

-10-

Home, Sweet ND Home

As it turned out Joe Kernan was the toughest guy I met at Notre Dame. Oh, there were a lot of tough guys on campus in the mid-60s. I remember a few of them from the football team. There was George "Mr. Clean" Goeddeke, Tom Regner and Kevin "Three Sports" Hardy to name just a few. On the basketball team there was Larry "Elbows" Jesewitz. As I recall doing play-by-play on WSND Radio, Elbows once fouled out of a game without scoring a point.

Joe Kernan was a pretty tough guy too on campus; after all he was a catcher on the baseball team. I think we had all of this macho stuff back then because, sadly, we were still a decade away from co-education. Guys have other ways to strut in front of women but when you are from all male litters, someone has to be the alpha dog. Most of us didn't have a clue how to impress the occasional young woman who would wander on to the campus at mid-day. As Father Hesburgh told me when I interviewed him just before his retirement: "I took pity on the poor St. Mary's girls who came to campus before co-education. It was like feeding time at the monkey house."

But of all those tough guys Joe Kernan proved to be tougher than the rest. Four years after graduation he was shot down over North Vietnam, captured and held prisoner in the not aptly named Hanoi Hilton. Joe never gave an inch, never told them anything other than what was required by the Geneva Convention. He came out nearly a year later as an American hero and went on to a distinguished career as Mayor of South Bend and both Lt. Governor and Governor of Indiana.

So Joe survived the Hanoi Hilton but he could not survive the Notre Dame Field House.

I lived in the Notre Dame Field House in the summers of 1965 and '66 and for the first semester of '66. Joe was the second of my three roommates, the summer of 1966. We had a great time even though we barely saw one another. To make ends meet, Joe worked as a night shift studio cameraman at WNDU and I worked early mornings signing on the radio stations. By the way, a special note to all you aspiring broadcasters out there, do not smoke unfiltered Camels if you are signing on a radio station at 5:30 in the morning.

Joe never made it through the summer. The end came in early August and I will let him tell the story.

46

"The sun is just coming up and I open one foggy eye and think I am having a dream. I shake off the cobwebs and open the other eye and it is not a dream. There on the windowsill six inches from my bed is a rat. Not just a rat but a rat that looked like it had been imported from the Bronx. It is so hot in there that we slept naked, so I grab a sheet like somehow this will fend off the rat and start screaming for you. As you are scrambling to wake up and come save me, I grab the string to the light bulb above my bed. The light goes on, the rat takes off like a rocket towards you coming in the other direction, I look up and a damn bat takes off from the ceiling and flies right by my head. Right then and there I make my decision, don't you remember my last words to you as a roommate?" "No I don't, Joe, there was way too much confusion and I don't like rats either." Said Joe, "I am outta here." And he was. Joe packed his bags and moved back into his old South Bend neighborhood (his family had moved to Washington D.C. but he wanted to stay but not with rats and bats) and lived in the basement of a former neighborhood widow.

So how did we get in the Field House to begin with? At the time many of the non-residence buildings had someone staying in them, quite often students. The reason we were told was for fire insurance purposes, the thinking being that if a fire broke out it would likely be spotted quicker if someone were in the building at all times. In theory that makes a lot of sense but, as I recall, it was probably more likely we would start a fire than spot one. I still vividly remember having a dual hot plate, small refrigerator and a toaster all in one multi-plug, but no dummies us, we unplugged everything prior to the semi-annual appearance of the Fire Marshall.

It did not take a lot of pull to get into one of those buildings, at least in the summer. Now the campus is alive year round but then the summer was down time and very few students wanted to stay. I was one that did because I had a shot at my first job in television in the summer of 1965. From almost day one at Notre Dame in 1963 I had been hanging around the Athletic Department. Hard to believe today but other than the football staff, which was housed at the Rockne Memorial building, the entire Athletic Department was in the basement of Breen-Phillips Hall! Legendary Sports Information Director Charlie Callahan took me under his wing and told me about a summer job in the sports department at WSBT-TV. Boy did I want that job. But there was a problem. I didn't have any money for a place to stay. So Charlie took me to Business Manager Herb Jones who put me up in the Field House, just a few feet from BP Hall. And what a deal that was because you did not have to pay a room fee and as time went on we figured out how to get a lot more for free too.

My first roommate that summer of 1965 was another Notre Dame legend, Cappy Gagnon. In all of the 45 years I have been associated with the University I don't think I know anyone who loved the place more. Once he came he was not going to leave as a student and even after years away he has now returned to campus as Special Events Security Director.

Like me Cappy was a blue-collar kid, at a time when there was still a place at Notre Dame for a lot of blue-collar kids. He got to be my arranged marriage roommate through Nappy Napalitano, Mr. Bengal Bouts. Nappy pretty much ran the place and in doing my research many of those who preceded us in the Field House were boxers.

Cappy worked three jobs to pay the bills. In addition to the Field House, he did campus tours from 8 to 2 and then worked the three to eleven shift at the unlamented Roseland Motel. So, just like Joe and me, we seldom crossed paths except in the dead of night and Cappy to this day loves to tell the story.

"The Field House was not meant for human habitation in the summer. It was ghastly hot. So hot that often both of us could not sleep, so we would get up and go to breakfast at 3 a.m. Back then finding anything that was open 24 hours was next to impossible, so we walked about three miles, avoiding even then the dangerous short cuts, to the Toddle House. We both loved baseball and that is how we passed the time, talking baseball. Only South Bend historians will remember the Toddle House. It was a classy greasy spoon just across the street from Memorial Hospital."

By the way, Cappy, it was the building and not the outside heat that made the place so unbearable. According to South Bend meteorologist and weather historian Rick Mecklenburg, neither the summer of '65 or '66 was abnormally hot.

There were no campus rules when you lived in the Field House, yet Cappy and myself, I think, were pretty good guys and caused little trouble. Of course we knew if we did we would lose our room and our jobs.

Cappy is convinced he probably saved my career choice, television news. I had forgotten most of this but Cappy has a steel-trap memory and I think he has it right. The job I wanted so badly was at WSBT as a film camera-man in the sports department but there were two problems. First, I had no idea how to shoot film and, second, I would have to drive the sports department car which was a stick shift and, truth be told, I never drove a stick in my young life. Cappy couldn't help with a camera—I was saved on that front by a wonderful man, WSBT Sports

Director Joe Pate—but Cappy "taught" me how drive a stick, sort of. Neither of us had a car so he set up two chairs opposite one another in the Field House and using his hands and legs showed me how it worked. And it did until I had to come to a stop and every time I did the news car stalled.

The two of us returned to our dorms for the fall semester and when we ran into each other on campus, we agreed, we were both bored by regular campus life.

By the next summer Joe and I started taking a few more chances than Cappy and I had.

We decided to let others enjoy the Field House with us. Sometimes this backfired

Joe remembers one story in particular.

"I come home at midnight from WNDU and even as dark as it was in the arena I notice a haze in the air. My first thought is that you finally started a fire with the hot plate, but no, you were fast asleep and not on fire. I couldn't find anything amiss so I went to bed.

The next morning trouble knocks on the door. It is Harold "Benny" Benninghoff who spent 25 years as the Athletic Department Maintenance Supervisor. Joe, he said, come with me, I have something to show you. Oh brother! There was a huge chunk taken out of Johnny Dee's basketball court. Did you do this Joe? No. Do you have any idea who did? Well, maybe. Who? Before I went to work I gave my key to two basketball players on campus for summer school who said they wanted to take a little extra practice. Well that was not the plan as it turned out. The basketball court was surrounded by a huge dirt track. The two basketball players fessed up. They took the Field House tractor on time trials around the court and finally lost control and crashed taking out the huge chunk. Coach Dee was not pleased and the next time we saw those two basketball players they were running laps around the court."

But what happened to me after Joe fled from the Great Rat and Bat Attack? I had no place to go and I was frightened. The Field House was a scary place alone at night without the addition of critters on the prowl.

So I went to Benny and asked if I could get a cat from the Humane Society. Benny is one of those laid back small town kind of guys, a man of few words, if you know what I mean. First he just looks at me, then a smile comes to his face and then he starts laughing out loud. "A cat? Have you seen the size of those rats? They will take that cat of yours, drag it out of the building and have it for breakfast on the steps of Cavanaugh Hall. Go get a dog with a loud bark." So I did, a collie that I named Patrick. If St. Patrick can drive the snakes out of Ireland then Patrick the dog could do something with the rats in the Field House. And he did. Patrick slept in my bed and the second he heard the distinct sound of skittering rats outside our door he went berserk. The rats took off to their holes elsewhere in the Field House.

Still we had to get rid of the rats for good and Benny came up with a plan. The two of us cleaned out every hardware store in South Bend of D-Con. Benny told me not to tell anyone because this had not been approved by the powers that be. We put the D-Con everywhere except my room because we did not want to kill the dog too. In two weeks nary a rat was to be found in the Notre Dame Field House.

Benny was a great guy and how he kept that old place—it opened in 1899—in shape was beyond me because its better days were long gone. Benny recalls a funny story told to him by Nappy. Bob Hope came to campus in 1962 to receive The Patriot of the Year Award. Keep in mind there was no ACC, no Stepan Center, so every big event was at the Field House. Nappy is taking Bob Hope through the building in the afternoon and Hope says to him, "What time do they let the horses in?"

By the fall semester of 1966 I was a made guy. Herb Jones and Benny told me I could keep the room and pick my roommate. I chose Gene Farrell. This article is dedicated to his memory. Gene was a real Chicago guy, you know what I mean? He knew how to get things done. As I mentioned, if you lived in one of the non-residence buildings you did not have to pay the ND room fees. But Gene thought we could do better than that and we did. First he talks a pretty young girl at St. Michael's Laundry into taking our clothes bags in a back door which is where we picked them up free of charge. Then he easily figured out how we got free meals. He tracked down dozens of students who either did not go to breakfast or possibly to lunch. He took their cards (no pictures on them at the time) and somehow in the age before copiers duplicated them. So we just went to lunch and breakfast like CIA agents with fake names and ate so much that dinner was not necessary.

Gene also taught me how to have fun with bats. The rats were gone so Patrick and the bats were our pals now. Gene said if a bat is giving you a problem by hanging on the bedroom ceiling, throw something at it and when it takes off, hit it with a tennis racket. If you hit it straight on, the bat is headed to the great bat cave in the sky.

One night Gene nails a bat and decides to get a little revenge. The football student manager's office was next to our bedroom. One of the managers was always giving us trouble accusing us of stealing things like basketballs, which was not true. We were only borrowing them until the end of the semester. The student manager was a real neat freak and when he left at night the only thing on his desk was a telephone. Gene takes the dead bat and puts it in the middle of the desk and covers it with a shoebox. We can't wait! At precisely 8 a.m. the neat freak manager opens his office. Now what would you do with an unexplained shoebox in the middle of your desk? Let me put it this way, the screams were blood curdling. He never gave us another problem and even asked us if we would like a free basketball. No thanks, said Gene, we are all taken care of.

The autumn of 1966 was an exciting time at Notre Dame. Our freshman year, 1963, we won two football games but here we were three years later watching Ara lead the Irish to a National Championship. You can only imagine just how BMOC the football players were that season, so big they could do just about anything they wanted as long as they did not get caught. Every Irish fan knows about Hanratty to Seymour but no one knows about Farrell to Collins. Now, I think, the story can be told because even Student Affairs must have a statute of limitations. A couple of the players talked the two of us into letting them and some of their teammates use the Field House late at night for basketball. It did not take long to get out of hand with the numbers growing and suddenly what we had was an indoor version of

Bookstore Basketball. One morning I get up to sign on those radio stations and I knew there was trouble right away. The door is wide open and the lights are still on and it got worse from there. The place was a mess and a large trashcan appeared to be filled with empty beer cans. I wake up Gene, call work and tell them I am sick, which in a way I was, and we went on a clean up bender. Somehow we made it before Benny, or even worse the neat freak student manager, showed up. And that is how Gene and Mike helped win a National Championship.

After that there wasn't much more to do, so I got married. Co-education was a decade away so co-habitation in the Field House was not an option.

The wedding was at Sacred Heart on December 26th. The bachelor party was Christmas night in the Field House. The wedding party all stayed with me. There was Gene and the late Don Nieman (ND Class of '67), Tom Murphy, who went on to serve three terms as Mayor of Pittsburgh, and another buddy from the Steel City, and Patrick the dog. Herb Jones stopped by with a case of beer and Benny even joined us for a while. We played cards and darts and then turned on all the lights and played HORSE on the official NCAA basketball court. We were having so much fun that we did not notice it had snowed. The campus never looked so beautiful before or since. Other than the priests, we were the only ones there and we decided to go for a walk in the pristine snow. As we came back you could see the light in the room in the northwest corner where I lived. I can still see that light gleaming off the snow to this day.

-11-

The Fabric of Our Lives

YOU CAN'T BUY IT, you can't wish for it, it just seems to happen. I have been blessed to be around Notre Dame for all of my adult life. In recent years I realized how much the University has become the fabric of my life.

Maybe I should have realized that earlier. After all, between my family and my wife's family we have four consecutive generations of Domers—my son Matt, my wife's father, her great-uncle and me. By the way, great-uncle Harold Lower played WITH Knute Rockne, 1912— you can look it up.

But what I am talking about has to do with more than a legacy. It has to do with trying to live your life in a way that would make the University proud. It can be something big like making a difference for others or it can be something you can do every day, like just being kind and helpful.

I see this all the time in hundreds of Notre Dame people (not necessarily all alumni) I have been close to through the years. Two of my compatriots on football game days come to mind. Mark Tulchinsky may have influenced more young lives in South Bend than anyone I know. And Rich O'Leary, the long-time director of Rec Sports at Notre Dame (and first lacrosse coach) was one of those people everyone looks up to and seeks their advice. But you can take Mark and Rich and multiply them by the X factor when it comes to Notre Dame.

I see it today in the current students. Working on campus a couple of days a week I have gotten to know dozens of students from all over the world. What a joy it is to hear them talk about doing something good for others with their Notre Dame education.

I am proud to be the Voice of Notre Dame Stadium but football is a game, life is not. If we can all leave behind a fabric from our lives because of Notre Dame, then it can be said we lived like a champion every day.

Mike Collins and Tim McCarthy

ND and Penn State: College football the way it was meant to be played.

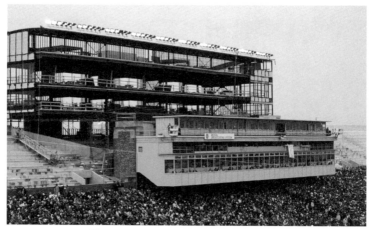

The new pressbox dwarfs the original.

Brian Boulac, a great ND coach and now a great spotter in the PA booth.

Tim McCarthy does his safety announcement
with Mike after the third quarter.

Jerome Bettis, Mike's favorite player while PA announcer.

The nuts and bolts of game day in the timimg booth. Late great ND guys Rich O'leary and Mark Tulchinsky are on the far right.

Mike and Melissa Collins after his induction into the Monogram Club

Mike Collins inducted into ND Monogram Club
on his 25th anniversary as PA announcer.

The Notre Dame Fieldhouse;
the two students lived to the far left of the main door.

The final game in the "cozy" original PA booth.

The first night game against Michigan with Musco lights.

Joe Sassano with Lou Holtz

Writers' Row in the original Pressbox.

Tim McCarthy peering out of old pressbox.

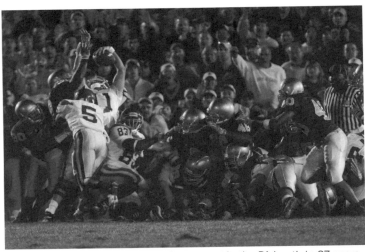

The "Bush Push," the most chaotic moment in the PA booth in 27 years.

PART TWO

by
Tim McCarthy

Getting home safe is like golf...
you need a good driver

-1-

Origins of the
Fourth Quarter Safety Message

The road might be rocky...
if you drive when you're stoned.

IT WAS IN 1952 that veteran trooper Steve Ranich became the first Safety Education Officer for Dunes Park Post District #1 that covered the nine counties of northwest Indiana.

Similar positions were also created in the other state police districts throughout the state. Now a sergeant, it was his duty to encourage and promote safe driving by every means possible. There was no funding available and the success of the program depended mainly on the initiative and ingenuity of each "Safety Ed" man, as we called them. They soon found that the success of the project was through a close working relationship with local police departments, the radio and newspaper media, civic organizations, industries, businesses, schools, and anywhere else preaching safety might make an impact. It must have helped because the traffic collision rate in Indiana began to show a reduction, particularly in fatal collisions.

Steve Ranich was a personable and convincing individual and ideal for his assignment. He came up with a

> Monkey around in traffic...
> and you may end up in a cage.

project of getting together with the University of Notre Dame and having a traffic safety message broadcast over the public address system to the thousands in ND stadium toward the end of each home football game. The university thought it worthwhile and gave it their blessing if Ranich would construct and personally announce each message. He did so and identified himself as "The Voice of Safety." That was the beginning of the safety message given during the 4th quarter of each Notre Dame home football game.

A few years later Ranich was promoted to First Sergeant and Executive Officer for District #1, and trooper Al Hartman was promoted to the Safety Ed post. Al was a good fit for the position. Having a very likeable personality, he was the trooper who was usually selected to give talks about the Indiana State Police or safety topics to civic and youth groups. Al was one of my training officers when I was new to the department and he became my friend and mentor both on and off duty for many, many years. As part of his new job, Hartman took over the 4th quarter safety messages for a few years.

In 1960, Ranich was promoted to be Commander of a new sub-post in Lake County and Hartman replaced him as First Sergeant at District #1. Soon after, I was promoted to sergeant as the Safety Ed officer for the nine county district. A day or so later, First Sergeant Hartman called me into his office to inform me that one of my duties was constructing and announcing the safety message at each home game and that there were two games remaining in the season. I hadn't thought about it until then. To help me get started, he told me the format he used was to open with, "May I have your attention, please," then identify yourself, and then give an appropriate safe driving message. His words that really stuck with me were, "Be professional and precise because if

Some drivers get in the doghouse...
because they take too many nips.

you muff one word, they'll laugh you right out of the stadium." That immediately caught my attention. An additional job I was given for football Saturday was to escort the visiting team to the stadium. It was the same routine for every game. I would meet the team and staff on game day at the Spaulding Hotel in Michigan City,

Indiana. They would arrive usually on Thursday evening. Friday they would hold a practice at Ames Field, which was, and continues to be, a nice stadium in that city. On game day, I would escort the two or three Greyhound buses that would carry them to Notre Dame. It was a red light and siren thing a good part of the way, but we stayed close to the speed limit and were very careful. It would not be good for anyone should the game be delayed because of a traffic mishap; particularly not good for the trooper responsible for the escort. Al Hartman gave me the route he used when he did the escort. It was a good route and there was never a problem. Four-lane highway all the way until inside South Bend where we would cut over to a neighborhood side street that was a little-known route almost direct to the stadium. At first I wondered what the residents thought when they saw a state police cruiser escorting Greyhound buses through their quiet neighborhood. Then I realized that they were likely familiar with the game day escort. Though long

Drive like a musician...
C Sharp or B Flat.

retired from escorts and the state police, I still use that route whenever going to Notre Dame, particularly on game day Saturday.

When arriving for the escort duty I would report to

the head coach or one of his staff. More often than not, the head coach would ask if he could ride with me. I first thought it was strange preferring not to ride with his team or assistant coaches. Then it became obvious that

 Those who have one for the road... may have a policeman for a chaser.

the coach simply wanted no distractions and to concentrate solely on the game as he rode to the stadium. They would sit up front with me and hardly ever say anything except to ask how long would it take to get there. Mostly staring straight ahead, it was like they were in another world. They seemed to have no interest in anything except the game. Once in a while an assistant coach would accompany the head coach. They seldom spoke to each other. It was obvious their minds were on nothing except winning against the Fighting Irish. Sometimes they did, most times they did not.

After arriving at Notre Dame sometimes the head coach would ask if I would like to watch the game from the sidelines with his team. That was very thoughtful. They were all nice men and gentlemen, even if they were trying to defeat the Irish that day. Being on the sidelines with their team would have been an interesting experience, but I had to head for the press box.

-2-

The Press Box

 You'll never find that bluebird of happiness... with too many swallows.

AFTER COMPLETING the escort duty, I would go up to the stadium press box located at the top of the west side of the stadium. It was a long climb if you took the stairs or you could take the only elevator that held no more than ten people if they were all crushed together. There was always a long line of people waiting for the elevator. That old elevator had to be the slowest in the world and it was not uncommon for it to stall. It actually was much faster to take the stairs if your heart could stand the climb.

That elevator was unpredictable. One time the Irish were playing Navy. At every game, both teams always have a handful of their coaches in separate parts of the press box to view the game from above and then phone the head coach on the field to recommend any adjustments they feel necessary. At half time, the elevator would be held at the press box level exclusively for those coaches so there was no delay in getting them to the main floor for a fast trot to the locker rooms and a half-time game plan consultation with their team and head coach. They have very little time and they move at full speed. Never make the mistake of getting in their way. If they bowl you over, they don't have the time to stop and apologize, or even pick you up. With halftime nearly over, the elevator would again be waiting for the coaches to take them back to the press box. At this particular game the elevator broke down while returning the visiting team coaches to the press box. After a short while it began working again. The coaches were not at all happy about being stuck on the elevator as the game was resuming and many wondered if it was not an intentional stall. It stalled once when I was on it and I prayed to God I would not be there forever.

That elevator was so slow that more than once I saw the press box coaches run all the way down the flights of stairs to the main floor, and on their return run all the

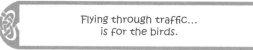

Flying through traffic...
is for the birds.

way back up the stairs. Even a few seconds is critical to them and their game plan. By chance I once happened to be on the elevator with three of the opposing coaches returning to the press box after halftime. I thought this is great because I wanted to eavesdrop on anything that might be said about the game. I wanted to hear some "coach talk." I was disappointed. On that slow ride up, they stood shoulder to shoulder, looked straight ahead, and did not utter a single word. They were three very

 Undertakers can tell you...
an accident is a grave situation.

intense men. It would be a foolish person who would want to jokingly suggest to those three that football is only a game.

The old press box was a class within itself, and a genuine piece of history for Notre Dame football lore. The structure was located at the top of the stadium, as is the present press box that was built during the stadium renovation. It looked like an add-on to the original stadium. The exterior and interior were very basic and spartan. It was for the working press only and always crowded. At that time, but it later changed, there was only one female present and she was a teletype operator. A pleasant red-haired lady, she provided the only charm among all those hard-nosed newsmen.

The press box main floor had, as I recall, three tiers the length of the building for the seating of the news people and sports writers. There was a small counter near the elevator where hot dogs and soft drinks were avail able and a small men's rest room was at the far end of the building. The red-haired woman had to take the stairs down to the stadium mezzanine level for the nearest ladies' room. With an inconvenience like that, it is small wonder the female gender sought equality in America.

 Driving is like ordering a steak... when you get home, be able to say well done.

Near the center of the press box was an enclosed stairway to an upper floor that had booths for the coaches and executive booths for visiting dignitaries and the like. My favorite place was the outside balcony that was midway between the two floors and accessed by a short open stairway on each side of the press box main floor. It was an open balcony that held television camera crews, radio broadcasters, news photographers, the stadium announcer booth, and a Red Cross team that monitored activities in the stadium below in order to best coordinate their people if Red Cross responders were needed for any emergencies. I liked the open balcony even on blustery chilly days; you were there with all the noise and hoopla of the game and an exceptional view of the stadium. There were no seats on the balcony. It was standing room only, but what a great view of the game. Everywhere in the old press box people were crowded shoulder to shoulder, but no one ever complained.

Entry to the press box was tightly controlled. Everyone entering had to be wearing a special press box tag. An usher stood at the elevator door and another at the stairway to check each and every tag. No tag, no get in! They actually checked for counterfeit tags, believe it or not. There were a few instances of someone trying to get in that way. Even though I came to be recognized by the ushers and was always in full state police uniform, they still would carefully check my tag. I didn't mind because I admired the way they did their job. I always maintained that the pope himself would be refused entry if he did not have a press box tag.

The press box ushers were fine gentlemen. They all had years of experience at the games before being placed in the press box. Those old timers could tell great stories about the press box and some of the games.

After I arrived at the press box my first time, I soon made my way to the PA booth. I was surprised to find the stadium announcer was someone I was already acquainted with, Frank Crosiar. Frank was the manager

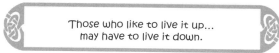

Those who like to live it up...
may have to live it down.

of radio station WSJV and a popular radio personality. For some time he did radio play-by-play broadcasting of high school basketball games in the South Bend area and was very good at it. To his listeners and others he became known as "Mister Basketbal." He is also said to be the person who coined the term "Hoosier Hysteria" in

If more people drive right...
there will be more people left.

referring to the Indiana basketball season. I met Frank several months before while doing some state police promotional work at his station. He was an easy man to work with. Briefing me on what I had to do, he told me there was nothing to it. He wanted me in the PA booth between the 3rd and 4th quarters. He would pick a time when there was a lull in the game, usually a time out, hand me the microphone and give me a cue when to begin the message. He told me not to pay attention to the crowd noise. I told him I was a bit nervous and hoped to do a good job. Frank said, "Don't worry, should you make a mistake I'll take care of it immediately." I asked how could he "take care of it immediately?" He said, "Very simple. I'll just shut the mike off."

Frank was fun to work with. He knew college football and what was going on down below on the playing field. He also was a hard-nosed Irish fan. An excitable individual, Frank would sometimes get so wound up during a close game that his hand holding the microphone would begin shaking so fast it's a wonder he didn't shake the mike to pieces.

Early in the fourth quarter there was a time out, Frank handed me the mike, I gave the safety message, made no mistakes, Notre Dame won, and I thought the day ended pretty well. One thing was obvious, however. It was hard to cut through the usual stadium noise at Notre Dame with a safety message. It made sense though that the fans were there for a fun day of football and not interested in a policeman asking them to behave themselves and to be careful on the way home. The stadium crowd had about as much interest in hearing a safety message from a police officer as they would for an anti-stomach acid commercial. There is no doubt it did some good to encourage safe driving, but not as much as I would have liked.

Having an accident is not the way to end the day... as a smashing success.

-3-

Press Box Stories

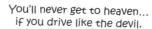

You'll never get to heaven...
if you drive like the devil.

RALPH (DUTCH) HENNINGS, a longtime photographer with the South Bend *Tribune,* was a regular on the press box balcony. He was there to take photos of the game. Dutch was well known to state troopers in northern Indiana, but not because of his photography. On June 28, 1938, he was riding on patrol with a friend of his, William Ray Dixon, who had been a trooper on the state police department for nearly three years. They were on Fail Road in LaPorte County taking a prisoner to jail whom Dixon had arrested as the result of a traffic accident. Along the way, Dixon saw a car stopped along the road with the hood up. Dixon stopped to offer assistance and walked up to the two young men in the car. When he asked who owned the car, one of the men stepped from the automobile with a gun and began to shoot point blank at Dixon. Dixon was unable to grab his service revolver because one of the bullets hit him in the

77

hand. Dutch Hennings, unarmed, scampered into a near-by cornfield to avoid getting shot. The men then jumped into Dixon's police car and fled the scene. The prisoner avoided getting shot by convincing the men that he was a prisoner on his way to jail. Dutch was able to get to a telephone to notify the state police post at Dunes Park and a massive manhunt was initiated. Dixon died two days later, but not before he learned the killers were captured, one dead and one alive who was later sentenced to death and executed at the state prison. Trooper Dixon paid with his life for trying to help someone he thought was having car trouble.

The stadium wall was lower than it is now since the renovation. From the balcony you could see an open field that was one of the stadium parking lots. As a game was being played, a person standing next to me gave me a nudge and told me to look over to one side of the parking lot. He said there was something that didn't look right. Sure enough, I could clearly see four young men

You may get grounded...
if you drive when you're high.

breaking into some of the cars. Dutch was nearby and I asked him to take a look. I also asked one of the ushers to contact the parking lot security. Then I had an idea. I asked Dutch if he had a telescopic lens. Dutch caught the idea, put the lens on his camera, leaned across the railing of the balcony and snapped several photos of the auto burglars. At the next game I asked Dutch how the pictures came out. He said he went to his photo dark

Safety First...
will make you last.

room, developed them, and they were better than he had even hoped. They showed the break-ins being commit-ted and clearly showed the faces of the thieves. He gave everything to the sheriff's department, which was able to arrest the culprits in short order. I told Dutch that I didn't have a medal for him, so I gave him a cigar.

At another game I learned there was a prince from a Middle Eastern country in the top floor executive booth of the press box. I had never seen a real prince before and wanted to get a look. A short time later I heard one of the ushers tell another usher to try and clear the aisle as the prince was on his way down the stairs to the el-evator. It was halftime and the main aisle was crowded with everyone taking a stretch. Soon, a man appeared at the stairway door who was not one of the regulars. He was about six-foot-three, an athletic physique, was very handsome, and wearing a tailored dark colored double-breasted suit with his hand inside the breast of the suit like Napoleon. He was a dashing looking individual.

Following him, was another six-foot-three guy, also extremely sharp looking, and with his hand inside his double-breasted suit like Napoleon. They looked like twins. Then I realized that they were bodyguards for the prince

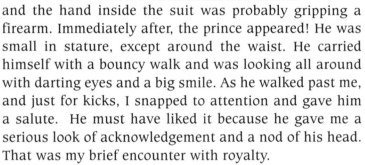

A heavy foot...
is a step away from jail.

and the hand inside the suit was probably gripping a firearm. Immediately after, the prince appeared! He was small in stature, except around the waist. He carried himself with a bouncy walk and was looking all around with darting eyes and a big smile. As he walked past me, and just for kicks, I snapped to attention and gave him a salute. He must have liked it because he gave me a serious look of acknowledgement and a nod of his head. That was my brief encounter with royalty.

It's always fun to watch the antics of some of the people in the stadium. One time it involved the police contingent of state, city, and sheriff's officers all seated together on sideline bleachers at the north end zone of the playing field. The great majority of them are Notre Dame fans, maybe even 100%. It was one of those games in which the Irish were having a tough time. The score was close. The Irish had the ball near the ten-yard line at the north goal line on the side of the field facing the police group. They were in a huddle getting ready to play the third down and hoping to make only a few yards for a first down that could eventually lead to a touchdown. As they broke from the huddle, a South Bend city police sergeant jumped out in front of the police contingent and with the antics of the best of cheerleaders he led the police in a rousing cheer for the Irish. It's possible the team heard it. The fans at that end of the stadium saw it and heard it. It got them laughing and cheering for both the police and the team. Well, the Irish made that first down and it eventually led to a touchdown. Maybe it was a time that cheering really helped. From then on, that South Bend police sergeant probably went through life telling anyone who would listen about how he once saved the day for a Notre Dame football team.

At a USC game I was standing in the press box balcony watching the pre-game activities and the like. Standing nearby was a cameraman setting up his camera. He turned to me and said, "Is it always like this? The noise?" I asked him what he meant, as everything

A drinking driver is like a gun...
both are dangerous when loaded.

seemed "as usual" to me. He told me that he was here from California to video the game, and had been in a lot of stadiums but this was his first time at Notre Dame, and he had never seen a crowd so worked up and the noise from the cheering was something else. I laughed and told him the cheering he heard was for the marching band taking the field, and when the team enters the field you're really going to hear some noise. The game the

Traffic after the game is no circus... so do not clown around.

California cameraman was getting ready to video was coach Dan Devine's legendary green jersey game. When the Irish burst out of the tunnel onto the field in those dazzling green jerseys, the stadium went crazy. Having some fun, I took a look at my new cameraman friend and said, "See what I mean?" He asked, "What in the world is going on?" I replied, "I could explain it to you, but if you're not an Irish fan you wouldn't understand it." The cameraman returned to California impressed. I was impressed too. USC was predicted to win big time but the Irish wiped them out, big time.

On the Thursday before that green jersey game, I was invited by the Sorin Hall students to say a few words at their outdoor pep rally. I was flattered to get the invitation. The students apparently were beginning to get a kick out of my ending the safety messages with a corny quip and wanted to know what this guy looked like. It was held on the front porch of Sorin Hall. Everyone was worked up for the coming USC game. Ken MacAfee, a tight end on the team who had gained a reputation for his incredible pass catching, was one of the players speaking at the rally. He and I had a conversation in which he told me how fortunate he had been with his football career from the time he was in high school and up to playing for Notre Dame. He went on to say that he had been able to do everything imaginable in football except for one thing. He said that during his time at Notre Dame his team was never able to defeat USC. It was obvious it really bugged the young man. The following Saturday during that fantastic green jersey game, he was a standout. He was catching anything and everything. At the Sorin rally when I shook hands with him, I thought what large hands he has. It's no wonder he can catch passes like plucking grapes off a vine. At coach Devine's green jersey game, All-American and future Hall of Fame athlete MacAfee caught eight passes and scored two touchdowns. The Irish won 49 to 19. Ken MacAfee got his wish.

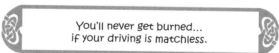

You'll never get burned...
if your driving is matchless.

Everyone gets excited at Notre Dame football games. The news people and sports writers included. There has always been an unwritten rule in the press box that cheering is prohibited. However, the rule is occasionally broken during a tight game by the pro-Irish members of the press. When this happens the guilty ones are chastised by John Lloyd, the longtime announcer of the press box address system, who dryly announces, "We remind you that the press box is for members of the working press and cheering is prohibited." Those words bring chuckles from everyone. You can loudly oooh and aaah and groan, but you better not cheer.

John Lloyd sometimes displays his own style of humor. The announcements on the playing field by the referees are piped over the press box speakers. The referees always give it in a stern and official style. At a game not too long ago the referee announced a penalty. It was, "Unsportsmanlike conduct. Defense. Fifteen-yard penalty." Forgetting to turn his microphone off, a second or so later the referee was heard to shout, "And you can't do that!" It brought a roar from the press box people. John Lloyd then announced, "We do thank the referee for his editorial comment."

 Getting your wires crossed in traffic... could be a shocking experience.

-4-

Interlude

 Half the trouble in traffic...
is caused by a fifth.

In November of 1957, I was directed to report to the Dunes Park Post by district commander Lieutenant Charles Sutherland. A gentleman by the name of Alexander Field from Chicago's WGN Radio and Television was with him. WGN had received permission from state police superintendent Harold Zeis to produce a radio show that would broadcast conversations between a state trooper and traffic violators that had been stopped. The traffic violator would not know the conversation was being recorded. There was nothing illegal about it because not in any manner would the violator be identified or the conversation be used against him in court. The purpose of such a program was to promote traffic safety by showing the senselessness of careless driving from the lame excuses of traffic violators, and it would be a weekly radio show by WGN. They asked if I would be interested in getting it started, and I agreed.

My assigned patrol area included highways US 20 and US 12, between the city limits of Gary and the Michigan state line, a twenty-six mile stretch. The two highways were the busiest in the state and notorious for heavy traffic, traffic law violators, and collisions, particularly during weekends. Traffic wrecks are no longer referred to as accidents, but as collisions because they are "caused" collisions and do not happen by accident. We always said that during the summer weekends everyone in Chicago goes to Michigan and everyone in Michigan goes to Chicago, and we're in the middle. It seemed that way. US 20 had the reputation of being known as Bloody Twenty in many newspaper and magazine articles. Veteran trooper Tony Perrotta and newspaper journalist Al Spiers wrote a story about the carnage on US 20 that appeared in the *Saturday Evening Post*. The area was ideal for the WGN project. In later years and after construction of the Indiana Toll Road and the Interstates, that same heavy traffic quickly evaporated from US 20 onto those better

 People who weave in and out of traffic... often end up in stitches.

and safer highways much in the way those same super highways made the Notre Dame football traffic easier and safer. US 20 had always been the most practical route between the Chicago area and South Bend.

Everyone was familiar with tape recorders that used large reels of magnetic tape, but portable hand-held tape recorders with cassettes at that time were something new. WGN gave me a small battery-powered Dictaphone

Drivers who pass on hills...
sometimes don't make the grade.

recorder with a microphone that was half the size of a penny box of matches, and a supply of cassette tapes. Dictaphone might have been the first to manufacture such a recorder. It was a unique item. The microphone would be attached to the uniform and the recorder carried on my gun belt or in a jacket pocket. It worked fine, except things like passing traffic noise and windy weather caused background noise. In two weeks I had enough of the recordings and took them to WGN for their review. They liked it and began putting the weekly half- hour radio show together. It was to be named "Signal 10." Signal 10 is the state police radio code for an emergency situation. WGN personality Carl Grayson was chosen to be the announcer and narrator. Carl had a precise and commanding radio voice and was perfect for the show.

One morning I was behind a car that was making a left turn from US 20 to go into Michigan City. I had been following the car only a short distance and noticed the driving was far from being up to par. Suddenly the driver made a left turn. The turn was far too wide and the car bounced over the curb and then back to the pavement. The car started to head into the opposing lane, but

You won't have a ghost of a chance...
if you drink too many spirits.

then abruptly cut to the right to stay in the proper lane. I turned on my red light and stopped the car. At first, I thought I had someone who had too much to drink. However, the driver was a sober elderly gentleman with his wife in the passenger's seat. I asked him for his driver's license. He told me he did not have a driver's license. I asked him why not? He said, "They won't give me one because I am blind." As the conversation went on, there was no doubt the poor man was blind. Not totally blind but blind enough that he could barely see his hand in front of his face. I never had one like this before. I asked him how in heaven's name did he get this far? He said, "Officer, to tell you the truth I couldn't do it without my wife. I keep it nice and easy and she tells me when to slow down or speed up a bit, tells me to turn a little this way or a little that way, helps me with the steering wheel in turning, and it all works out pretty well." I asked him if it wouldn't be better and much safer if he simply let his wife drive? He said, "What? Oh no, I couldn't do that.

She's a terrible driver!" Unbelievable, but it's a true story. I had the Post phone his son who arrived shortly after with another driver to take them and their car home.

Another time on US 20 I was directly behind a car and the sole occupant was doing a fine job of driving. The man in the car, who appeared to be a good-sized person, was driving exactly at the speed limit, staying in his own lane, and had all the marks of a good driver. Suddenly he began jumping around in his seat, shaking his head, working his shoulders back and forth, and appeared to be shouting. Then when he began beating the dashboard with his fist, I decided it was time to stop him and find out what was going on. I also was thinking, he's a big dude and I hope there's not going to be a problem. I walked up to the car and the driver gave me a curious look and asked, "What's the matter, officer?" I told him that's what I'd like to know, that he was doing a great job of driving until he suddenly started bouncing around, shaking his head, shouting, beating the dash-

Driving when you're half high…
is not the way to get up in the world.

board with his fist, and is he having some sort of a problem? He started to laugh and I mean a belly laugh. He said, "Please let me explain, officer. I'm the pastor of a church in Chicago and I was just practicing the sermon

I'm going to give this Sunday and was getting all worked up over it. I get very emotional when it comes to serving the Lord." I told him, "Well, pastor, I'll tell you right now that your congregation is going to love it because it looks to me like your sermon is going to be very exciting." Before we parted he invited me to attend the service, but I told him that I have to work Sundays, just like he does.

No one is more honest than a child. I stopped a man for driving 75 mph in a 55 zone. His young son was in the back seat. The man claimed I had to be wrong because he was a safe driver and was not one iota over the speed limit. He was very emphatic about it and to the point of being argumentative. Suddenly his young son spoke up and said, "Daddy, the policeman is right. I was watching the speedometer and it was almost at eighty one time." The man's objections were over. I smiled at the boy and told him, "Well, that was nice of you, young man, I'm sure your dad appreciates your concern." I then asked the father to step out of the car and kidded him that it seems

The highway is not a racetrack...
so any horseplay is a bad bet.

I had a witness. He looked at the ground and had nothing to say. I told him I had every intention of writing him a ticket, but because the comment by his youngster was no doubt embarrassing and punishment enough, he could

go on his way with a warning. I also suggested he treat his son to a hot fudge sundae or better because he certainly saved him the expense of a traffic court fine. Did he deserve a ticket? Of course he did, but I also thought how upsetting it might be to that little boy when he realized

Pressing your luck in traffic…
is not the way to iron things out.

he sided with the policeman who gave his dad a speeding ticket. Later I had to chuckle as I wondered how his wife was going to take it after the youngster told mom about daddy and the policeman and how fast daddy was going with their little boy in the car.

It reminded me of the time I stopped a woman who was speeding. A little girl was sitting next to her. When I told her I stopped her for speeding she said, "It's an emergency, officer. My little girl needs to go to the bathroom, and quick!" The little girl then announced, "But mommy, I don't have to go to the bathroom."

The "Signal 10" radio show ran much longer than the three months I predicted. It became very popular. Some of the other troopers provided a good helping hand by making recordings for the show from time to time. At its peak, with WGN and the Indiana State Police working together, more than forty-some radio stations in Indiana broadcast it weekly, also fifteen other stations throughout the United States, two English-speaking stations in Central America, and one in South America, and an unexpected plus was that it was broadcast over the Armed Forces Network in Europe from their radio base

You may be at the end of your rope...
if you tie one on.

station in Germany. I normally spent most of my patrol time in and around the area of Michigan City. A soldier who returned from the Cold War in Europe was a Michigan City lad who told me he never missed a broadcast over the Armed Forces Network because he was familiar with most of the locations mentioned on the program and it made him a little homesick for home.

"Signal 10" ran for almost thirteen years. WGN discontinued the program after seven years, but the state police continued to service the other radio stations by sending them replays of the program for another six years. From a public service viewpoint it was quite a success for WGN. In 1959, "Signal 10" won the prestigious Alfred P. Sloan Award, the nation's highest award for excellence in public service broadcasting and traffic safety. The award was presented to WGN general manager Ward Quaal and a delegation of state troopers, including myself, during the annual Sloan Foundation dinner in New

York. Alfred P. Sloan was a past president and CEO of General Motors Corporation and an active and respected philanthropic individual. WGN was the first Chicago station to win the award, and then went on to win it twice again for an unprecedented three consecutive years. In 1960 and 1961, two new programs accompanied "Signal 10" in the award, the "WGN Trafficopter," and "WGN Traffic Central."

The Trafficopter radio program began shortly after the Signal 10 project. It consisted of periodic radio broadcasts by a police officer in a helicopter of traffic conditions in the Chicagoland area in the morning and late afternoon. The purpose was to keep motorists traveling to and from work informed of the general movement of traffic, any delays or backups, road and weather conditions, and suggested detours whenever necessary. This type of traffic reporting was a first for Chicago. The person selected to do the reporting was Chicago police officer Leonard Baldy. Len was great at it. He was sharp

The amount of collisions caused by drinking drivers... is staggering.

looking, had a good voice, a quick mind, and was a credit to the Chicago Police Department. Len also was the first Chicago police officer ever to use radar as a tool against speeders. Radar was a new idea for traffic law enforcement and Len was the first officer in the world to make a speeding arrest using radar. We became good friends and often had lunch together when I would bring my work into WGN.

Listening to his broadcasts I was amused when he would occasionally slip in a quip during his reports. I thought it added a little extra to the reports and told him so. Len typed out a few of the quips for me in the event I might have a use for them sometime. I filed them away, but stored the idea in the back of my mind.

WGN had Len coordinating another project that as I recall was originally Len's idea. It was to be a four-state reporting of traffic conditions during the summertime oneach Sunday afternoon and early evening when traffic was at a peak. It was set up to involve the Indiana, Illinois, Michigan, and Wisconsin state police departments with each giving periodic spot traffic reports from their state to be broadcast on WGN. It was to be called "Sunday Traffic Central." WGN was a powerful radio station and had a

 Drive like a happy doctor... have a lot of patience.

substantial listening audience in each of those states.

On May 2, 1960, WGN phoned me with some devastating news. During a routine flight over Chicago the helicopter used for the traffic reports developed a malfunction in the rotor blade and crashed, killing both Chicago police officer Leonard Baldy and the pilot, George Ferry. I lost a very good friend and Chicago lost a dedicated police officer, the likes of which will never be seen

> The driver who thinks he's King of the road...
> may get crowned.

again. One Chicago police official said that most Chicagoans did not know the name of the Superintendent of the Chicago Police Department, but they all knew officer Len Baldy and who he was.

I was asked to take over Len's coordination of the four state police departments for the "Traffic Central" production. It worked out well and mostly because Len had already done the groundwork. It was another successful public service program by WGN.

The helicopter traffic reports continued. After a temporary assignment of officers, a permanent replacement was Chicago police officer Irwin Hayden. Irv and I became friends and exchanged stories and ideas. Irv also had a seasonal television program on WGN that was a traffic safety quiz show involving students from area high schools. During one season I worked with Irv on the show as a guest moderator; a totally new experience for me, but Irv made it easy and pleasant.

On August 10, 1971, again came the devastating

news of another WGN trafficopter crash. Irv and the pilot, David Demarest, were killed when the copter, flying at a low altitude was blown into high electric tension wires and crashed to the ground. In my years as a police-

 Drivers that have close shaves... often get clipped.

man, I lost some good friends and acquaintances "in the line of duty," but none bothered me more than the tragic deaths of Len Baldy and Irv Hayden.

Len Baldy's son Tim was two years old when he lost his dad. In later years he began researching his dad's life and accomplishments. It resulted in writing his dad's biography in a book titled *Chicago's Finest*. It's good reading about a dedicated police officer. Tim Baldy's book also resulted in two separate streets leading to the WGN studio being renamed Len Baldy Way and Irv Hayden Way by the city of Chicago in memory of the two. My wife and I were there for the dedication ceremony and it brought back memories to us of two fine men, good family men, and wonderful friends.

Remember the line often said by John Candy as he portrayed an Irish-American Chicago policeman in the classic movie film *Only the Lonely* with Maureen O'Hara, "Sometimes it's good to be a policeman"? Well, maybe it is sometimes...but certainly not all the time. During our time with WGN, none of us ever received extra pay, stipends, or the like, for what we did or those many extra hours of work. We did it because we believed it was part of our obligation as police officers sworn to protect and serve the public. But I do admit, we enjoyed doing it. It was quite an experience.

Never get bent out of shape...
keep your driving straight.

-5-

Safety and Smiles

 Too many cold ones...
could put you on ice.

Aᴛ ᴛʜᴇ sᴛᴀʀᴛ of the 1961 home season I was looking forward to giving the 4th quarter safety messages the entire season. When doing it for the first time the year before, there were only two games remaining in the season. The messages at those two games went well, but I found it was going to be difficult to break through the usual constant noise of the stadium, even though stadium announcer Frank Crosiar tried to slip me in at the best time possible, which was generally during a timeout. I also thought that in trying to promote traffic safety it might be beneficial to steer away from a typical dry and mundane-type safety message to something that would attract some attention. That's when I began thinking about the humorous quips Len Baldy used occasionally while giving his trafficopter reports over WGN radio.

From the half dozen quips Len gave me a few years before, three of them seemed to be ideal for the football games. My idea was to try one and see how it would go. At the first game of the season I was ready with a message cautioning the football fans about the risk of drinking and driving that ended with a quip. Just into the fourth quarter of the game, Crosiar picked a break in the action and handed me the mike. Frank noticed the crowd was unusually quiet because of a discussion between the referees and mentioned it was a good time for the announcement. Frank gave me the cue and I gave the message on drinking and driving that ended it with, "Remember: The automobile replaced the horse...but the driver should stay on the wagon!" Crosiar started laughing and so did Ted Wilson, his spotter. There was also a reaction from the crowd below that was a combination of laughs, groans, and boos.

Fortunately, and because the stadium was on the quiet side at that particular time, it went better than expected so I decided to try it again. At the next game the message regarded driver attitude ending with, "Some drivers are like steel...no good if they lose their temper!"

Weaving in and out of traffic...
Can make you a basket case.

That also went well, including the groans and booing. Thinking I might be on the right track, I did the remainder of the season using the quips and found the stadium noise beginning to quiet down so they could hear the quip. Many of the quips were so corny that the booing increased, particularly from the students. I never thought I would appreciate being booed. It didn't bother me because while the stadium crowd was quieting down they

 Following too close...
is not the way to make ends meet.

were listening to the entire safety message to hear what the quip was going to be. Better than ever anticipated, the quips became a surprisingly good gimmick in getting the stadium crowd to quiet down enough to where they listened to the focus of a message that encouraged safe driving. That was the objective, reminding people to think about the importance of getting home after the game, safe and sound.

Going into the third season with the quipped messages, I noticed the students were not booing as much. In fact, the cornier the quips, the more they seemed to like it. I even detected a few cheers. People began asking where I get the quips. That's an easy question to answer, anywhere I can. Actually, nearly all the quips come from listening for a play on words during the year, jotting it down, and as the football season begins, trying to put it together into a quip that can relate to traffic safety.

The hardest part is finding quips that can relate to a specific traffic situation. Once in a while someone will send me one in the mail. A big surprise came when I received one from a student at Notre Dame, the first of a few received over the years from students at both Notre Dame and Saint Mary's College.

If you drive to beat the band...
you may end up playing a harp.

The best received from a Notre Dame student was during the 2006 season. I was in the Joyce Center before a game as the iconic Irish leprechaun, cheerleaders, and pom squad were performing for and working up the crowd to cheer for the Irish. I met the leprechaun during a break in their routine, a senior named Kevin Braun. The leprechaun for the season is always a senior who is selected by a panel of judges for being at the top of the list after a rigorous and competitive selection process. Kevin mentioned he had a quip he thought I could use. It was aimed at drivers who had too much to drink and could end up getting arrested. It even had a football theme to it. It was a good one and I promised Kevin it would be used later in the season. His quip was, "If you drive when you're blitzed...you may get sacked!" It brought a good response from the crowd and as I looked down on the field at leprechaun Kevin, he appeared very happy.

Listening to radio and television talk shows and even commercials are good sources for sometimes catching phrases that can be worked into a quip. An example was the long-time wine commercial by the legendary actor Orson Welles who would end the ad by saying, "The fine wine that improves with age." I converted it into, "Remember: Fine wine that improves with age…is only sour grapes in traffic!" It went well, but afterwards I began to think about the possibility of repercussions from the wine industry. That bothered me, because I always try to avoid even a remote possibility of a quip being negative or offensive, or infringing on anyone's rights or feelings.

Though giving the safety messages during the fourth quarter at each Notre Dame home game for so many years, I still get nervous about it at each and every game. I never forgot the words of my predecessor and mentor Al Hartman, "Muff one word and they'll laugh you out of the stadium." I always thought I did fairly well, but there was one game I'll never forget. It was late in the season in mid-November and the weather was horrible

Safety first…
makes you last.

on that Saturday. It was freezing, but hardly anyone left their seat even though the Irish were leading by a good margin. Typical dyed-in-the-wool football fans were in the stadium that day. The stadium PA booth in the old press box was almost totally open-air. There was no heat in the booth except for a very small electric heater. That little heater only put enough warmth on your feet to let you know how cold the rest of your body was. It was so cold that the people present in the usually crowded open balcony area were only those who had to be there. To make matters worse, the PA system was cutting off and on at times, much to Frank Crosiar's aggravation. When my time came, he handed me the mike, gave the cue to begin, and all went well until I got to the word "never." I was shivering so bad it came out, "ne, ne, ne, never." One of the troopers later kidded me about stuttering the "never" word. I told him, "I did not stutter the word. It was a vibration caused by the PA system cutting in and out from ice that had gotten into the wiring system." It was a good try, but I don't think he believed me.

After using the quips four seasons, I began to wonder if it might have run the course and it was time for a change. It was for no particular reason except thinking

 Driving under the weather could mean...
a fine today, the cooler tomorrow.

the quips might be getting too much on the humorous side for a safety message. I decided to return to the more formal safety message at the next game. The stadium quieted down as I went into the message and when it was over, they stayed quiet. They were waiting for the quip that never came. Later several persons asked what happened and if the PA system went out. When I told

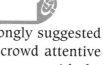

Our purpose is not to give you the needle... only that you get the point.

them why there was no quip, it was strongly suggested (by my boss) that to have the stadium crowd attentive to the safety reminders, it might be best to stay with the quips. So after that advice, the quips continued.

The traffic safety message runs approximately twenty-five seconds. A day or so prior to the game, I type it out on a 3x5 index card. I have always used the same format, and every word to be said is printed on the card. I never counted how many of the messages I have given—it's been quite a few, but I continue to be as nervous as the first time I gave one. No one likes to make a mistake before 80,000 plus people. I'm so paranoid I even type my name on the card to avoid any possibility of messing that up. An example of the 3x5 is:

MAY I HAVE YOUR ATTENTION, PLEASE.
This is Tim McCarthy for the Indiana State Police.
Fans…please keep your trip home as safe as possible
By driving with caution, courtesy, and common sense.

Take your time, stay alert, and above all, do not mix Drinking and driving.

REMEMBER: DRIVING HALF LIT...
IS NOT VERY BRIGHT!

It's wise to be prepared for any eventuality, such as the weather. If rain is predicted for game day it is not unusual to have sunshine instead. Occasionally a game begins in nice sunny weather, and then halfway through the game an unexpected rain begins falling. As for snow during a home game, there hasn't been snowfall for a long, long time. That's because home games are not scheduled as late in the season as they once were. To keep ahead of the weather, I always have an extra card handy in the event of rain and another should there be a surprise snowfall.

Something not a surprise, but certainly unusual, was the first night game in the history of Notre Dame stadium. This was during the 1982 season scheduled home game against Michigan that was to be played over prime time television. Because the stadium never had lighting for the playing field, Musco Lighting of Oskaloosa, Iowa, was contracted to bring in portable lights that were bright enough to facilitate the televising of the game. Musco brought in trucks, each carrying a generator and a telescoping beam that raised a lighting unit high above the stadium. Six of the trucks surrounded the stadium.

106

It was something to see. The Musco lights certainly did the job. The truck units put out a great deal of noise from motors and generators as one walked past them, but inside the stadium there was no noticeable noise. The playing field was illuminated as well as the best daylight. A local television station measured the intensity of the lighting on the playing field and determined that it was brighter than the lighting in their studio. Another story was that the referees asked to have the lighting reduced during the game because the players from both teams were complaining about excessive brightness. In later games that season when artificial lighting was necessary to ensure ample lighting for prime television daytime or night, only four Musco units were used instead of the original six. I know because I counted them. A little-known fact is that Musco Lighting received an Emmy award for their success in nighttime lighting for NCAA football games at Notre Dame, Ohio State, and Bearcat Stadiums for prime time television.

 Anyone who thinks a little rain is not dangerous... is all wet.

I was retired from the state police by that time, but in talking with my old comrades it was obvious the police were concerned about additional traffic problems that could occur after a night game because the after-game traffic would be driving during darkness rather than during daylight hours. However, the day ended with no serious problems from that first night game at Notre Dame. In fact, many thought there were fewer problems. The police believed it was due to an extra measure of caution by each and every driver. That overall driver attitude was another example that Safety Pays.

If you drive to beat the band...
you may have to face the music.

-6-

Notre Dame Rallies

Drivers with an axe to grind...
often fly off the handle.

I ALWAYS THOUGHT it would be fun and exciting to attend a Notre Dame pep rally. I had never been to one. I assumed there was only one rally, the big gala rally held before every home game. However, that is not the case. There is rally after rally at Notre Dame during the football season. Students informed me that the big gala rally always held on Fridays, the night before a home game, is known on campus as the "official" rally. Other rallies held by the student dorms or their organizations on campus are known as "unofficial" rallies, better known as "hall rallies." They are conducted solely by the students of a particular Hall, and with the permission of the university.

Getting to be a regular at the games with the fourth quarter safety quips, I was invited to be one of the speakers at a rally held by the Senior Bar on campus. This would be my first experience at a rally. I had no knowledge of the "Senior Bar" or what it was, or what they wanted. The Senior Bar at that time was a large old

109

house that was allowed to remain standing after the acquisition of some acreage procured by the university and permitted to be used by the senior class for various activities. I was assured it was only for seniors, and there was no unlawful dispensing of alcoholic beverages. So, I agreed to say a few words and hoped for the best.

The problem was trying to decide what those few words would be. I didn't think they wanted to hear a spiel about safety at a pep rally that was supposed to be a fun thing. Since every Irish football fan is familiar with the old recording of Knute Rockne's locker room pep talk to his team before a game, I thought it might be humorous to give a Rockne version of how he would brief a state police unit as they readied themselves to work traffic at a game. In my job as a safety education officer for the state police I did a great deal of public speaking, but nothing like this. When I arrived for the rally, it was raining. It was an outdoor event and I thought it might be cancelled. It was not cancelled. The senior commit-

Drivers that play leapfrog in traffic...
often croak.

tee worked so hard on the rally there was no thought of a cancellation. Eventually I was led to the podium by crawling through an attic window as we made our way onto the sloping asphalt shingle roof of the building.

There was still intermittent rainfall. I thought, what am I doing here? One slip could mean falling off the roof and how would I explain it to my superiors? What was the line, "My Kingdom for a horse"? I would have given

Not using a shade of caution...
could be curtains.

away my paltry kingdom for an umbrella and non-skid sneakers that evening. The other speakers did their thing and then it was my turn, drenching wet in full state police uniform. I did my Rockne routine and it went fairly well. There were laughs and even some applause. They must have liked it because they made me an honorary member of the Senior Bar and said I was welcome any time. It was a crazy night, but a lot of fun with those seniors. That was my first exposure to one of the "unofficial" rallies.

I previously mentioned the experience with the Sorin Hall rally. What is interesting about the unofficial rallies staged by the various student halls is that the rally is not only for their hall residents, but the entire student body is invited. There is always attendance by hundreds of students at these outdoor rallies. Each hall has a fierce competitive spirit with the other halls, but when it involves Notre Dame as a community, it is wise never to stand in the way of their support for each other.

I always remembered a remark made at the Sorin rally by one of the assistant coaches. He told the students, "Notre Dame is more than an institution, Notre Dame is a way of life."

John Broderick, a professor at the Law School who

You won't have a ghost of a chance...
if you don't have the right spirit.

was known as the Chief, phoned me one day and invited me to say a few words at his law class rally. It was customary with the Chief to conduct a rally at the beginning of his class on the Wednesday prior to a home game. I can't recall how much time I spent putting together an outline on what I was going to say, because I really wanted to do a good job for Chief Broderick and his class. I came to the class totally prepared. I met the Chief, a bandy rooster type individual, before the class began. He told me where to sit, make myself comfortable, and then he disappeared. The law students filed in and took their seats. Suddenly the music of the "Notre Dame Victory March" resonated wall to wall over the speaker system as Chief Broderick stormed into the classroom waving an Irish shillelagh. He was wearing a kelly green hat, an ancient oversize green plaid sport coat that was adorned with a multitude of assorted Irish football pins and a couple of bumper stickers. The applause, cheering, and shouting from the students was enough to shatter eardrums. The Chief quieted them down, introduced me and told his class I had a few words to say and to listen carefully. It led to more applause, cheering, shouts, and so forth, and it didn't stop. I was unable to say a word. Then the Chief raised his hand, quieted the class, and said "Thank you, Sergeant McCarthy, you may sit down." I was stunned. I never said a word. Then Chief introduced two football players he had invited. Each stood up to say a few words and the same thing happened. They weren't able to say a word. The Chief sat them down and wielding his shillelagh he immediately led the class in a rousing Notre Dame cheer. After that, the speaker system again blasted out that rousing rendition of the Victory March. Then it suddenly became quiet. Next was the grand finale of playing the school anthem, "Notre Dame Our Mother," as the law class sang along with it, linked arm in arm. The rally was over. Lasting about fifteen minutes, it went bang, bang, bang. What a great

What's at stake is prime...
and that's not a bum steer.

routine by the Chief! No one was able to say anything except the Chief and that is how he always conducted his rally. Looking back, it was the most spirited Notre Dame rally I ever attended. It involved only a classroom of law students, was no more than fifteen minutes long, and the only speaker was one principal character named!

Dillon Hall has a tradition of holding a rally on the Thursday before the first home game of every season. It's quite a rally. Dillon Hall sets up a large outdoor stage and for an hour before the rally there is entertainment by either a rock band or a DJ as the students begin to gather. Soon the gathering is in the hundreds. The rally begins with the emcee taking the stage to get things started. Dillon residents begin pouring out of the dorm hall cheering, shouting, and running throughout the crowd in their specially designed rally T-shirts. The leprechaun is there with the cheerleaders and pom squad who give a performance.

The football coach makes an appearance, usually straight from the football practice field, to the delight of the students, and gets a great ovation. Some of the players show up to say a few words and joke around with the crowd, and the students love it.

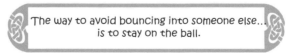

The way to avoid bouncing into someone else... is to stay on the ball.

In the middle of all this, the men of Dillon wear a variety of outlandish homemade costumes, give skits that involve anything from world politics to everyday doings at Notre Dame and eventually to the coming football game. The skits are funny and no doubt the result of much preparation. It is said they begin planning everything some four months prior to the rally.

Somewhere in the skits is always a fun reference to

The reason we hammer at safety...
is to keep you from getting nailed.

the Dillon Hall rector since 1997, Father Paul Doyle, a Notre Dame graduate himself. A native of Virginia, he has a southern drawl that is as long and lanky as he is in stature. A gentle and considerate individual, he is one of a few men I know who can get his point across without being critical. When privately listening to the Dillon residents speak of Father Paul, their respect and affection for him is obvious. For the past few years, Father Doyle has also been the football team chaplain for the home games and is always on the sidelines.

For the past several years I have been a regular speaker at the Dillon rallies. I don't do much except give a typical foruth-quarter-style message that reminds everyone to be careful during the football weekend and then end it with a quip aimed at the coming game; such as,

> *"Remember: On game day the Irish are going to shine...*
> *While the Spartans get polished off!"*

You never know what's going to happen at Dillon. At one rally, basketball coach Mike Brey made an appearance. After his remarks he suddenly leaped off the stage head first, diving into the arms of waiting students who

 Old-fashioned horse sense...
is always stable thinking.

caught him. After coach Brey, Father Paul came on stage to say a few words. Then suddenly, this long lanky priest dived off the stage and was caught by the students. I was next in line to do my thing, and I couldn't help but wonder if I could make the same dive and survive. Better judgment prevailed over temptation, however. I visualized the students all stepping back, like Moses parting the Red Sea, leaving only the cold hard earth catching me. It is stored in my mind as one of the things I always wanted to do, but knew better.

The official rally held in the Joyce Center basketball arena on the Fridays before every home game is no doubt the most spectacular. In recent years the emcee has been Chuck Lennon, the tireless and energetic long-time executive director of the Alumni Association. He gets things moving fast and furious and the rally begins. The place is packed with 12,000 plus football fans and the free tickets are at a premium. If you don't arrive early enough to get one, preferably a day or so before the rally, then you might be out of luck. When the Notre Dame Band marches in playing the Victory March, goose pimples and shivers run up your spine if you're a Fighting Irish fan. A unique thing is that you hear the band approaching, and to your surprise they appear in their casual street clothes. Their uniforms are held at the ready for the game the next day. If the rally is during Halloween week, many of the band members dress in Halloween costuming which is a novel treat for the fans.

There is always a good selection of speakers at the rally, anywhere from popular celebrities to legendary athletes. Often there is a football team from years past holding a reunion at Notre Dame during game week, and they seem as excited as though they are going to play one more time for Notre Dame. The leprechaun, cheerleaders and pom squad perform and work up the crowd. The climax comes from words by the football coach and a couple of the players. The rally lasts about one hour and it ends with the band playing and the students linked

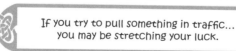

If you try to pull something in traffic...
you may be stretching your luck.

arm in arm singing the school song, "Notre Dame, Our Mother."

I have been at the rally a few times to give quip laced safety messages that are always narrowed down to a quip relating to the coming game. One that brought a good response was when the Irish played Pittsburgh, or Pitt as it is called. It was:

> *Remember: The game tomorrow will be a*
> *bowl of cherries...*
>
> *because the Irish know what to do with the pits!*

Any of the rallies are fun to attend, and it's a great way for a football fan to get excited about the game. During Charlie Weis' first year as coach, they decided to hold a special rally in the open-air Notre Dame stadium. The Notre Dame Security Police told me that the attendance for the rally exceeded 45,000 people. No one needed a ticket, there was room for everybody.

Notre Dame Alumni Clubs began requesting a recorded quip message that could be used at rallies they conducted for away games in their specific area, particularly if it was a bowl game. They preferred something that would relate to the coming game. A quip for a Cotton Bowl game held

When there is congestion...
you must keep a clear head.

in Texas took some thinking. Finally, it was focused toward Texas having strict laws regarding wrongdoing and the quip was:

> *Remember: In Texas they don't **cotton** to*
> *lawbreakers!*

118

It's likely a wedding reception could be interpreted as a family rally to wish the bride and groom long life and years of happiness. Martin Falkenberg, a Notre Dame graduate and friend, who at one time was in the market-

 Trying to shoot through traffic... may bang up your car.

ing department of the Seattle Supersonics and later with the Boston Celtics, gave me a phone call with a request. He was getting married. The planned wedding reception included a guest list of many ND alumni. Marty asked me if I could send him a recorded quip message to be played at the reception for old times sake. It was something different, but Marty was accommodated. Apparently it went well because Marty later sent me a Boston Celtics basketball autographed by their legendary coach, Red Auerbach. It was a pleasant surprise.

Since then other quips have been requested for ND alumni wedding receptions. The most recent was for a bride and groom who were both alumni Irish Marching Band members. The quip was given a marching band theme:

> *May you always dance to the same beat,*
> *and play to the same tune!*

Or maybe it could have been:

*Health and happiness in your married
life together…
And always C Sharp or B Flat!*

If you have a hot time in the old town tonight…
you may end up in the cooler.

-7-

Retirement...almost

When you bank on *safety*...
it's a *lifetime saving.*

IN 1978, I stepped into politics. I filed for and was successful in being elected as the Sheriff of Porter County and was to assume the position on January 1, 1979. That meant I had to retire from the Indiana State Police after twenty-five years of service. The one regret I had was leaving the assignment of giving the fourth quarter traffic safety messages.

Edward (Moose) Krause was the athletic director at the time. Moose Krause was one of the most admired men ever at Notre Dame and he eventually earned the nickname, Mister Notre Dame. Among many things in his life, he was an All-American in both basketball and football while at Notre Dame, head basketball coach for six seasons, later the football line coach, and then ultimately serving as athletic director for over thirty years. Excellent reading for any sports fan about this man's extraordinary life is in *Mr. Notre Dame,* a biography by Jason Kelly.

I mentioned to Moose Krause that I would be leaving. He said he was sorry to see me go, thought I had done a good job, and that it was OK with him if I would care to continue doing the messages. My boss expressed the same and asked me to continue as a representative of the Indiana State Police. I cheerfully agreed and have been doing the quipped messages ever since.

My wife, Carole, was already a long-time member of the sheriff's department serving as Jail Matron for the female prisoners. I met her when she was a young lady working in the county clerk's office. One of her duties was to bring court papers to the judges in the various courtrooms. I had arrested a man for manslaughter and was in the courtroom during the trial sitting next to the deputy prosecutor, Al Pivarnik. Carole walked in and she immediately caught my eye. I asked Al who she was. He told me, and asked if I would like to be introduced. We were introduced, I phoned her a few hours later for a

Careless driving is like borrowing money...
it's always touch and go.

date, she accepted, and seven months later we were married. And what happened to our intermediary? A while later Al Pivarnik was elected as the county prosecutor, served several years as prosecutor, and ended that career in his life when he was appointed a Justice of the Indiana Supreme Court.

When people ask me how I met Carole, I tell them I met her at a manslaughter trial. I always receive a strange

Get the best mileage home...
by not driving half tanked.

look and then have to tell the full story. A few years later, retired state trooper Ed Buchanan was elected sheriff and Carole joined the sheriff's department as bookkeeper. She stayed there for forty years working under several different sheriffs, including me.

After serving my terms as sheriff, I decided to retire completely. After about three months of that, I began to get very bored. There are only so many things to fix around the house and then you have to scrape for things to do to keep busy, and I'm not one to sit and watch the television all day.

The county assessor resigned shortly after she went into her third term of office to pursue another endeavor. I received a call asking if I would consider being appointed to fill the vacancy. The thought of that kind of work intrigued me. I tossed my hat in the ring for it and was appointed. It was an entirely different type of work than what I had been doing most of my life. After a month of ing people, and now I have to tell them what they can expect to pay in taxes." The job was challenging however, and that is what kept me there. I must have been doing a decent job, because I was re-elected for two more terms. I served almost twelve years as county assessor. Once again things went well. An exceptional office staff helped get it done.

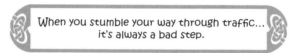

When you stumble your way through traffic...
it's always a bad step.

-8-

Mike Collins and Crew

Motorists that drive too hard...
often get arrest.

I NEVER ATTENDED NOTRE DAME. I never have been an employee of Notre Dame. I cannot speak as an expert on Notre Dame. The only thing I can tell about Notre Dame regards the experiences I have had with that great school. When I relate something about Notre Dame, it is how I see it and how I feel about it. Am I biased about the school, yes I am. And I'll say one thing emphatically, whatever I have seen done by Notre Dame, in my mind it has always been done the right way and it was the right way.

Stepping into the PA booth at the beginning of the 1982 season, I found there was a new stadium announcer. Frank Crosiar retired after years of service to Notre Dame. Frank did a fine job doing the play-by-play scenario for the stadium crowd over the years and I always admired his work. Being the stadium announcer is not an easy job. It requires professionalism and expertise. Frank had both those qualities and the personality to go with it.

The new announcer was Mike Collins. I did not know him personally, but I was aware of his longtime career as a television news personality in the South Bend area. Mike is a Notre Dame graduate, Class of '67. After a brief meeting in the PA booth, I watched as he got into his first game. If he was nervous, he certainly didn't show it. He prepared himself well, knew what he was doing, was accurate and articulate in announcing what was happening on the playing field, and seemed totally focused on doing an exemplary job for Notre Dame. You would have thought he had been doing it forever, he was that good.

After watching what goes on in the PA booth, it doesn't take long to realize that the stadium announcer has to master many demands. It's much more than just watching the game and telling the stadium crowd what's happening. He has to keep his eyes on the playing field every single second, or he's going to miss something. He and his spotters can't take the time to discuss a great catch by a receiver or the sack of a quarterback by a tough lineman,

Be a joker in traffic...
and you may get decked.

because they can't afford to miss the game action moving into the next play. There is no phone or radio communication from the referees on the playing field to tell the PA booth what is happening on each play, so the announcer has to tell it as he sees it from high above the playing field, and it's best to be accurate. One advantage the announcer has is being high above the stadium and having a perfect overall view of the game below. Sometimes he

 Dents on your car...
make a bad impression.

will notice something the referees might miss, but it is seldom the referees miss anything. He never mentions a possible referee miss on the PA system, but it amazes me how he or his spotters can catch it. A time-out on the field allows for a swig of water and a quick look around, but not for long. Any time-out for the PA booth often means delivering a special announcement about some after-game event, giving notice of a future or current event on campus, or to plug some charity. When a time-out is called, the stadium announcer immediately swings into the message, and occasionally they are lengthy. Sometimes messages are on notes given to the announcer on the spur of the moment and he is expected to deliver it flawlessly, which Mike always seems able to do.

With thousands of vehicles in the parking lots, there is an occasional spur-of-the-moment announcement that always brings laughs, except from the owner of the car:

Your attention, please. Will the owner of
a gray Buick, license plate Illinois 123456,

127

immediately go to your car in the parking lot.
The doors are locked... the lights are on...
and the motor is running.

After my experience with a spur-of-the-moment item is when I began to appreciate Mike Collins' ability to deliver those messages without hesitation, and with perfection. He does not have the time to review and rewrite a message as I did, he just happens to be a great ad-libber.

At our first meeting, Mike told me he was familiar with the state police traffic safety messages and would work me in at the best possible time. And that he does. In fact, he takes great pains at it. He hands me the mike, usually during a time-out, I wait until he gives me the cue, and then give the message. Should the game suddenly resume, or the band start playing, then I give the mike back and we wait until another break in the game. A good time to give it is between the third and fourth quarter immediately after the traditional 1812 Overture by the Notre Dame band. I have the mike in hand, Collins is ready to cue me, but then if the visiting band fires up, it's back to square one with Mike watching for another time. It is not unusual for that to happen.

Not long after he began as stadium announcer, Mike went from using a hand held mike to what's called a headset. It's a framework fitting over a person's head

128

with the microphone placed in front of the mouth. It gave him the freedom of both hands. It also meant that when Mike was ready for me, he had to remove the headset and I would put it on. It was a bit cumbersome. One

 Avoid bottling up traffic... by not driving half corked.

time we switched the headset back and forth five times before I could break in with the safety message. In the new press box Mike still has the headset, and now there is a separate hand-held mike for me or anyone else that might prefer using it, such as a visiting band announcer when doing his band's halftime performance.

I have often been asked at what time during the game do I like best for giving the safety message? That is a very easy question to answer. I like it best, and look forward to it, when it's late in the fourth quarter and Notre Dame is ahead by three touchdowns and appears to have the game wrapped up. It is even better if it's immediately after a touchdown by the Irish. When a game gets that Notre Dame victory momentum, I believe I could give the corniest quip ever and still get a good reaction from that pro-Irish stadium

In his first years on the job, Mike's spotters in the PA booth were Ted Wilson, who had been with Crosiar for many years, and Joe Sassano, a Notre Dame graduate in 1955, who had been with Crosiar only the year before. Previously, Sassano had been the head football coach for nine years at all-boys Catholic Weber High School in Chicago. After that, he returned to Notre Dame and for a few seasons did the color commentary from the press box for WNDU-TV at the games, and later on the on-the-field commentary for the Mutual Radio Network. Joe knows his football. His job is to tell the statistics of each play to the announcer, as the yards gained or lost on a play, length of a pass, and anything else he deems important. The stadium announcing operation is one of close teamwork

In the succeeding years, Ted Wilson eventually retired. Collins and Sassano remained, doing a splendid job for the stadium crowd from that cramped and outmoded PA booth. Then there was the rumor of expanding and rejuvenating the stadium. Everyone in the press box would vote Yes for that project!

Things can really explode...
if you drive when you're bombed.

-9-

New and Improved

Acting like a comedian...
could become a smashing performance.

AT THE BEGINNING of the 1997 season, the newly renovated Notre Dame stadium was open and ready for football. Everyone was looking forward to it. No one was disappointed. It appeared that every nook and cranny of the original Rockne Stadium was improved and rejuvenated. The addition to the stadium was even better. What we always called the Press Box was now a media center, even though all us non-conformists still refer to it as the Press Box. In my mind, one of the best innovations was the replacement of that old slower-than-a-turtle tiny single elevator that could only service three levels with two modern elevators that service five levels. Each one of those can carry almost three times more than old slow poke could. The new elevators now carry more than only the media people. They not only carry fans that would rather ride than walk up the ramp to the upper part of the stadium, but also the handicapped that have a special section in the stadium. A new feature that is not noticed by most people is that the elevator operator now has a seat. I always felt sorry for the usher manning old slow poke because he had to stand during every trip and continually hear complaints about *his* elevator. It was so slow that the usual comment was, "Well, do you think we're going to make it?" I remember one usher who replied, "I don't know. The problem with it breaking down is that we never get any notice when it's going to happen." Most of us on board laughed; but actually, it was true.

Everyone has memorable events. My most memorable event about the new elevators was seeing the great and legendary fighter Muhammad Ali step aboard. It was the first time I ever saw the man. The elevator was getting crowded and he was backing in to make room for everyone else. He happened to back into me and stepped on my shoes. He turned to me as if to excuse himself. Before he could say a word I said, "Perfectly all right, Champ. No problem whatsoever." He was well past his prime as

Safe drivers get the cheers...
by avoiding the booze.

a professional fighter, but in no way would I ever want to tangle with the great Ali. Later on I saw him on the fourth or Media level of the press box during halftime. He was sitting on a chair surrounded by several people, all wanting his autograph. Quite the gentleman, he was patiently signing each and every request, and the best part is you could tell he was enjoying it. The thought that crossed my mind was, I wonder if he would autograph the top of my shoe?

 When traffic becomes thick as fleas... don't let it bug you.

As you might imagine, the increase in attendance at the renovated stadium greatly concerned the police. 21,720 more seats meant a substantial increase in traffic. It's hard to calculate an absolute number, but a conservative estimate is at least 20,000 vehicles would now be rolling into the South Bend area opposed to the previous 14,000. This does not mean that they all park at the ND campus. Many choose school parking lots that offer parking as a fundraiser. Some leave the car at their motel or hotel and take a taxi or bus to the game. Many homeowners near the stadium offer parking on their driveways and lawns for a price, and always have a yard full of cars. Some fans park on streets several blocks away and walk to the stadium.

It takes a total of two hundred police officers from the various police departments to handle the security and traffic at the home games. Controlling the congested traffic is not an easy task for the police. They must closely follow the overall traffic plan, stay on the ball, and do everything possible to keep traffic moving smoothly and safely. The most difficult location in my mind is at the main entrance to Notre Dame, beginning at Angela

A sleepy driver...
can become a wake.

and Notre Dame Avenue and extending all the way to the reserved parking areas. Much of the football traffic funnels down to this location. Each driver has to be certain to get into the proper lane for his specific parking lot. The police help the driver by glancing at the sizeable parking lot "hang tag" displayed through the windshield and guiding him into the correct lane. Most of these are season ticket holders and know which lane they should be in, which makes it easier for the police. This area is manned by a large contingent of South Bend city police, and they do a fabulous job of coordinating the traffic despite some very difficult conditions.

An excellent change in the traffic pattern resulted when Notre Dame opened an entry gate for general admission parking directly across from the Indiana Toll Road exit on State Road 933, also known as Dixie Way or Michigan Street extended. The new gate saves motorists exiting the toll road or approaching from the south at least four miles of very congested traffic on game day. It not only affords the motorist time and convenience, but it also reduces the traffic at State Road 933 and Cleveland for the state troopers working that busy intersection. All the general admission traffic from the toll road has to do now is cross State Road 933 to the parking gate entrance. State troopers are also at that intersection to regulate the traffic for safe crossing.

In all, the increase in traffic due to the expansion of the stadium has not caused any overwhelming problems, mostly because the university and police departments were prepared for it.

My first time in the new press box facility, I went directly to the PA booth which was titled Stadium Announcer. Now in an enclosed room with heating and air conditioning, the announcer crew sits behind a full-view sliding glass window that can be open or closed, depending on the weather elements. I have never been there, however, when the window was closed during a game. The announcer crew prefers the window open

 Don't let what strikes you most about Notre Dame... be another car.

because you can better feel the spirit of the game. To the left of the crew is a large window to the adjoining room in which one can see the technical staff in the stadium sound room. Collins can immediately get their

135

attention by tapping on the window. To the right is another window that extends a view into a statistics room and further across to the next room where one can partially see the NBC Sports set with Pat Haden doing the color commentary of the game and Tom Hammond giving the play-by-play action.

During the 2007 season, NBC Sports televised to their national viewers all my traffic safety messages. It was extra work, but a good experience, and they are nice people to work with. I enjoyed it and hope it might have done some good to promote traffic safety.

If you pass by the media center entry on the west side of the stadium, you will see two large white semi tractor trucks and trailers parked inside a chain link enclosure. They belong to NBC Sports. The first time inside the one trailer, I could not believe my eyes. I can only describe it as a mobile media center. Every square inch was in use and crammed with video monitors, sound and editing equipment, and other equipment of which I had no idea what

You won't be taken to the cleaners...
if your driving is spotless.

it might be. There was a sizeable staff inside, all doing some sort of work, and this was a day before the game. I always thought that everything necessary to televise the game was in their room in the media center overlooking the stadium, but that is not the case. The trailer is like a cross between a nerve center and a studio. Televising a football game, I found, is quite an operation.

Another member of the Collins' crew is Brian Boulac

Tearing up the highway...
could be the end of the road

who focuses on the defensive actions of both teams. He is presently an Assistant Athletic Director and the general manager of the Joyce Center. A former Irish end, he is a veteran of many years at Notre Dame on the football coaching staff, among other coaching and athletic responsibilities. For four years he was head coach for the women's varsity softball team and guided them to four 30-win seasons.

I try to be in the PA room before the game begins because I enjoy watching the Band of the Fighting Irish make their entrance. It is the oldest college band in continuous existence in the United States. To an Irish fan it is electrifying and the best part of game day other than the game itself. Jon Thompson, a long-time radio personality with his talk show "JT in the Morning" over WSBT in South Bend, is the announcer for the band. Jon is spectacular in his presentation as the band takes to the field. He has a dynamic voice that is unique in delivery. When you hear his voice announce, "The Band of the Fighting Irish," you know you are in for something special. And that's exactly what you get. The band's first number is always the classic "Hike, Notre Dame," as they march down the field doing their renowned hike step.

The trip home will be heavenly...
if you drive like an angel.

And when they play the "Notre Dame Victory March," it brings many a tear to those Fighting Irish fans in the stadium. It is emotional and it certainly gets everyone ready for Notre Dame football.

When I began the safety announcements in 1960, the band was less than half of what is now, with it's 380 plus members. I never realized Notre Dame had that many musicians. Later I learned that the number of musicians at Notre Dame is surprising, and being selected as a member of the band is the result of a very competitive process. Those who do not make it are encouraged to try for the concert band and jazz band.

In 2006, Dr. Kenneth Dye, the band director, asked me to participate in the band's annual CD that year. They intermixed some of the quip-laced safety messages with their usual football game music, plus a few other numbers. I thought it went well, and the band's music is great. They titled the CD, "May I Have Your Attention, Please" which is the lead-in for the safety messages.

I often watch the band's halftime show from the PA room. If there is a visiting band, it's always fun to stay and watch their performance. Recently a visiting band announcer had laryngitis so bad he was worried whether or not he could get through his band show script. The man's voice was so bad that Mike Collins offered to do the show from the script. That was both considerate and brave of Mike, not being able to review the script in advance. The man was determined to do it though. I usually carry a roll of cough drops in case I get the dry throat bug. I broke the roll in half and didn't have to ask twice if he thought it might help. He took two instantly. He did his show and got through it in good form.

Second to the Band of the Fighting Irish, I have to say that USC does fairly well. A couple of years ago their band announcer, who is very good at it, said to me, "I understand you're a policeman?" Then he laughed and said, "This is what I do in the real world." He flipped out his badge showing me he was a Los Angeles police detec-

Those who drive like the wind...
may blow it.

tive. I wished we had more time to talk. How he became connected to the USC band, I have no idea.

South Bend city police sergeant Al Deroo is a good friend of mine. He has been with the SBPD for more forty-six years. He loves the job, and when he does retire he probably will leave claw marks on the station door as it will be that hard for him to leave. He has worked the Notre Dame games for more than thirty years, with the last twenty on the sidelines watching over the visiting team and visiting band if there is one. He likes the traffic safety quips. We generally see each other sometime before each game and I always have to tell him what the quip line is going to be. Now, the USC band plays almost nonstop during the entire game. A bit of exaggerating, but it seems that way. At one USC game, I told Al what the quip was. He thought it was a good one. I mentioned to Al that it should go fine, except every time the USC band is here they always start playing as soon as I get into the message. Al said that he could take care of that for me. I told him the USC band was not that big a deal, and not to fuss about it. Sure enough though, Al diplomatically talked to the USC band director about it

 Drinking and driving...
is an arresting situation.

and thought everything was taken care of. Between the third and fourth quarters, after the Fighting Irish band did their 1812 Overture, I went into the safety message. I had said no more than a few words when the USC band cut loose, and they were louder than usual. I am sure I know what happened. It's likely the USC band director thought he was not going to let some Indiana policeman on the sidelines tell him how to run his band. Al told me

 The road to court is not a freeway... it is expensive.

all about it at the next home game. He was still peeved, but it gave us some laughs.

I spend most of my time at the floor level of the media center where the sports reporters and journalists are seated. There are also people there from the sports information department. The SID people gather statistical data and do communications and media work. This sports writers arena is guided by the talented hands of John Heisler who is the Sports Information Department director at Notre Dame, and a very busy man on game day. Heisler's assistant is the very capable Bernadette Caferelli. Bernie never sits and is always moving around taking care of this and that and anything else that needs attention.

At the end of each quarter, Sports Information provides a service I first noticed at the old press box. In only a minute or so after each quarter ends, their staff is distributing to every sports writer a complete statistical rundown of the game quarter, and it includes al most everything necessary for a sports news story. How they get it out that fast is a wonder, but they treat it as merely a routine. The data no doubt eliminates a lot of note taking. It allows the sports reporter to concentrate more on

Always keep your train of thought...
on the right track.

the highlights of the action of the game, which makes for a more colorful story. It's quite a service for the press media.

As in the old press box, the media center continues to have the "regulars." One I always enjoy is Joe Doyle, the South Bend *Tribune* Sports Editor Emeritus. Joe's been around a long time and he knows Fighting Irish football like the back of his hand. Though not a Spring chicken, he has a mind that's as sharp as a razor and a memory like a records vault. He would have made a great police detective. There is nothing more enjoyable than to sit with him and listen as he relates a few of his stories. He continues his writing, including a sports column in the *Irish Sports Report* publication. It's the first thing I turn to. Joe always has an interesting story, and you often learn something new.

Former coach Gerry Faust is a regular, as he attends most of the home games. The man truly loves Notre Dame. Energetic as ever, he moves around and seems to know nearly everyone on a first-name basis, or at least makes them think so. And many, many go out of their way just to step over and say hello to Gerry.

One of the most incredible stories I ever heard about Notre Dame accountability came from a regular in the press box named Ron Athey. Ron was the assistant director of Notre Dame Food Services. Ron and I first met on the open balcony of the old press box and we became good friends. One day we had a conversation about the accountability of the many concession stands at the home games. Ron told me there was very controlled accountability and related an example. He had Food Services begin conducting an internal audit every year. One season, out of approximately 200,000 hot dogs sold by the concession stands, the audit could not account for twelve hot dogs. Yes, twelve missing hot dogs! Now, twelve out of 200,000 you would think would simply be written off and ignored as insignificant. But it was not insignificant by Athey's standards. He ran it down and

 Trying to paint the town red tonight... may give you the blues tomorrow.

discovered that one of the packages of twelve hot dogs had been erroneously mislabeled as smoked sausages. He solved the matter of the unaccounted-for hot dogs.

The same year, out of approximately 200,000 paper

cups they had forty-three paper cups unaccounted for. Though retired, it wouldn't surprise me if Ron Athey might still be working on that one. This man didn't mess around.

Safety is food for thought...
and that's not baloney.

-10-

Ushers

 That fine wine that improves with age... is only sour grapes in traffic.

I ALWAYS THOUGHT the ushers rated at the top of excellence as Ambassadors of Good Will for football fans attending the Notre Dame games. As you pass through the gates to enter the stadium, the first thing you might hear from an usher is, "Welcome to Notre Dame." It kind of makes you feel at home. I've heard many a person from far away and rooting for the visiting team say, "You know, in all honesty, Notre Dame is very nice to its visitors. We don't have that in other stadiums." That's quite a compliment from people who wanted their team to whip the Irish.

The person who supervises the ushers is Cappy Gagnon, a Notre Dame graduate, Class of 1966. He has been the Coordinator of Stadium Personnel since 1995. A noted baseball historian, he is the author of *Notre Dame Baseball Greats* which is good reading for any sports fan, particularly those who like baseball. Cappy also has a notable background as a police training executive for the

145

Police Foundation in Washington, D.C., the Los Angeles County Sheriff's Department, and he also served as technical services manager for the Olympia, Washington, police department. Cappy has received many commendations for his work with government agencies, including one from the Los Angeles County Board of Supervisors for his work on their Blue Ribbon Commission for the Homeless. He also was a supervisor at a firm that provided security for thirty prominent figures in the entertainment industry. One task he had was to be security escort and provide the advance work for more than 100 venues of Cher's 1990 World Tour.

There are 857 ushers that work each home game. Unbelievably, they are from twenty-four different states. Incredibly, they receive no pay except the ones who work the entry gates, and that's because the gate ushers are unable to watch the game. Many of them have been ushers for years, many years. They simply enjoy being a part of Notre Dame football.

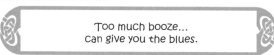

Too much booze...
Can give you the blues.

One such usher is Manny Oliveira. I met him at the 2009 The Shirt Unveiling event the day before the Blue & Gold game. He has been an usher for the past ten years at every home game, plus the Blue & Gold games. Where does he live? He lives in New Bedford, Massachusetts. He and his wife drive to South Bend the day before the games. He told me the first game he ever saw at Notre Dame was in 1946 when they played Army, and he fell

 You may be carving your tombstone... if you chisel in traffic.

in love with ND. I asked Cappy Gagnon if by chance he knew Manny Oliveira. Cappy knew him well, and said he's one of the best they have.

Manny told me a story. He ushers in Section 7, which is near where the band is seated. He was looking around his section and happened to notice a girl who was crying. He first thought she might be ill. He walked over and asked if anything was wrong, and told her he noticed her crying. She thanked him for his concern and said she was fine. She went on to tell Manny that all her life she wanted to see Notre Dame play football. This was her first time in the stadium, and she never dreamed it would be so thrilling. Hearing the band play and all the other excitement, it completely overwhelmed her and brought her to tears she was so happy. As they talked, two band members happened to pass by, one was carrying a football. Manny stopped the pair, told them the story of the girl, and got the band kids to walk over and have her pat the football for good luck. They did just that, and had a few words with her. With that, the girl completely broke down she was so thrilled. Manny wondered if he did the right thing. There is one happy girl who thought he did.

The ushers keep a sharp eye out for anything that goes amiss in their section. If a problem occurs they can't handle or there is an emergency, they know how to get a quick response by professionals, such as the police, medics, or fire department. If someone appears unruly or does not comply with the stadium conduct rules, for minor incidents they are told about it with the suggestion that the stadium rules be followed. If the conduct continues, there is usually no second warning. The person is immediately escorted out of the stadium.

Handicapped fans, such as those in wheelchairs, are given special considerations. Now that there are two elevators on the press box side of the stadium, and one other on the opposite side, the handicapped don't have the trauma of getting up a flight of stairs or ramp. On

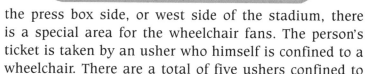

Those who drive when they're fractured...
never get the breaks.

the press box side, or west side of the stadium, there is a special area for the wheelchair fans. The person's ticket is taken by an usher who himself is confined to a wheelchair. There are a total of five ushers confined to wheelchairs who perform that task. Cappy Gagnon also has twenty-five ushers assigned as "pushers." The pushers move the wheelchairs about or to the restroom. If a chair-bound man is there with only his wife, she would

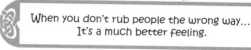

When you don't rub people the wrong way...
It's a much better feeling.

be unable to take him into the men's room. Notre Dame thinks of everything.

The gates into the stadium are closed until one hour before game time. Before the gates open, if you looked inside the stadium you would see the ushers gathered together at their specific section being briefed by their section leader. This is to keep them abreast of everything that is expected, any changes, and for questions and answers.

The ushers at the five gate entrances for the stadium hold their briefings near their assigned gate. After the briefing at Gate D, and just before they open the gate, it has become traditional for the ushers to gather together as a group and face the fans waiting to enter. Then as a choir they sing, "God Bless America." It delights the waiting fans and all others who are passing by. It's a nice patriotic touch for game day and the ushers enjoy it.

Any time there is a personal emergency in the stadium, the ushers notify the medical services. It could be a

149

heart attack, someone passing out, or someone who had a fall and was injured. Trained medics and other assistance are quickly dispatched to the location. The emergency is monitored and coordinated by the University Medical Services Outreach unit from their room in the press box that provides a generally good view of the stadium.

Ruth Ann Heberle, assistant director of Medical Services Outreach, coordinates fifty American Red Cross volunteers who serve as responders to the incidents. There are three first-aid stations in the stadium, two on the lower level, and one on the upper level. Those staffing the stations include six physicians who volunteer their services, and six registered nurses. If you walk past the stations and get a glance inside, you will see that there is seldom a lack of patients. The Red Cross responders use golf carts when it is necessary to transport those with minor injuries or illness to the aid stations. Ambulance service to the hospital for serious cases is by

Drinking drivers are not very funny...
but they can still crack you up.

the South Bend Fire Department. The ambulances are on standby at the stadium and manned by fire department medical teams. The medical outreach unit even has a van to transport the minor ill or injury cases, and family, to their car in the parking lot.

The university fire department also has equipment on standby at the Fighting Irish stadium to save response

When highways are wet...
the driver should stay dry.

time should there be an emergency. I always get a kick when I see the one fire truck that has lettering on the back stating, "Fire Fighting Irish."

There is a large room with entryways both on the outside and inside of the stadium that is used as a stadium police station. The South Bend Police staff it for use by all the police departments. It also has a temporary lockup cell. The police do make arrests at the games, mostly for excessive drinking or unruly behavior. After the initial reports are completed, those persons are transported to the county jail.

A police unit everyone likes to watch, especially the youngsters, is the Sheriff's Mounted Unit. They spend much of their time patrolling the parking lots. A mounted unit is ideal for patrolling large areas because they sit high on the horses and have much better visibility than a foot or vehicle patrol. When kiddies see them, they no doubt think that's what the sheriffs looked like in the old Wild West days.

Rain during a football game is something that is aggravating for the fans, but not unusual and most will stay in their seats and endure it. Weather that could be dangerous though, is something Notre Dame does not

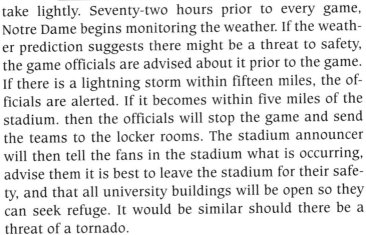

The best part about being alcohol free...
is you never have to pay for it.

take lightly. Seventy-two hours prior to every game, Notre Dame begins monitoring the weather. If the weather prediction suggests there might be a threat to safety, the game officials are advised about it prior to the game. If there is a lightning storm within fifteen miles, the officials are alerted. If it becomes within five miles of the stadium. then the officials will stop the game and send the teams to the locker rooms. The stadium announcer will then tell the fans in the stadium what is occurring, advise them it is best to leave the stadium for their safety, and that all university buildings will be open so they can seek refuge. It would be similar should there be a threat of a tornado.

There are not many places where eighty thousand plus can gather for a day of fun and excitement and be as safe and as well cared for as they are at a Notre Dame football game. Let me note an old Irish saying, "You are as safe as if you were in your mother's arms."

In my thirty-three years as a police officer I have

pulled duty at many mega events, and attended many others as a spectator. I cannot recall ever seeing medical aid and security services as well prepared, coordinated, activated, and equipped as they are at Notre Dame. It is remarkable. Even more remarkable is that much of it is accomplished with volunteer workers. They like to be part of Notre Dame football that much.

Don't shortchange yourself...
by not driving with any sense.

-12-

The Quips

THE SUCCESS OF USING quips at the end of each safety message still amazes me. I had only hoped the quips would do the job of attracting attention to the actual safety message. I had no idea the stadium would become as quiet as it does, listening to the entire message simply to hear what the quip was going to be. That was the purpose, creating a safety message interesting enough where everyone would listen and realize that the most important part of their day was getting home, safe and sound. All I can say is that the quips are a gimmick that worked.

Over the years I have responded to requests from other universities and even an NFL team who wanted to initiate the same quip-laced message at their games to promote traffic safety. There were also inquiries from high schools and a few industries. They were always given a few of the quips and suggestions how to put everything together. One university wanted to give one during every quarter of a game. I told them it was overkill and it would work best by keeping it to one message only and near the end of the game. How many of them carried through with it and how it went, I never heard. What works at Notre Dame may not work as well elsewhere, but it's nice to know they wanted to copy Notre Dame.

There have been many requests for copies of the quips. If for a worthwhile safety project, I would always send a few, but never all of them. There was one person who would periodically ask for several quips at a time. After I learned he used them in his business of advertising promotions and charging for it, that was the end of it for him.

Following are nearly all the quips used at the Notre Dame games so far, forty-eight seasons in all. Anyone who would like to use them for some safety project is certainly free to do so, and good luck. I do have some suggestions. As you review the quips, there will be many that at first may not make any sense. The plan should be to find a quip that fits in with the topic of the message you want to give. In other words, if the topic is about excessive speed, use a quip that relates to speeding, such as: Drive like lightning...and you may crash like thunder. If you use a variety of driving errors in the topic, and use a quip relating to drinking and driving, then make certain the drinking part in the meat of the message is the last item mentioned before the quip, and emphasize it because it then relates to the quip much better. Keep the message in your style of speaking and avoid fancy or complicated words, because they can get you in trouble. Keep it plain and simple, and it will be received better. In giving the message, project your voice, be articulate, and concentrate on reading the written message as you speak. You might even underline the words you want to emphasize so the emphasis is not overlooked.

I have always used the same format over the years, as the following example:

MAY I HAVE YOUR ATTENTION, PLEASE.
THIS IS TIM McCARTHY FOR THE
INDIANA STATE POLICE.

FANS... getting home safe after the game
requires careful driving and no mistakes
in traffic.
And don't forget that *any* amount of
drinking impairs *your judgment and
your ability.*
Remember: alcohol may make you feel
exhilarated...
But you may not be able to *pronounce it!*

I have to mention that I am very grateful to those who have taken the time to send me an occasional quip, and in particular those from the students at Notre Dame and Saint Mary's College. I am also grateful to the University of Notre Dame and the Indiana State Police for allowing me to give the safety messages for such a long time. And needless to say, I am most happy for all those in the stadium crowd who get home after each game, safe and sound and without a scratch.

Notre Dame Fourth Quarter Traffic Safety Quips from Tim McCarthy

The automobile replaced the horse...
but the driver should stay on the wagon.
Many drivers are like steel...
no good when they lose their temper.
Don't be a traffic surgeon...
someone who is always cutting up in traffic.
If you kid around in traffic...you may end up as the goat.
Drivers who bend their elbow too much...
often miss the bend in the road.
Drivers who pass on hills...are not driving on the level.
Getting behind the wheel...doesn't make you one.
Highway comedians never enjoy...their biggest hit.
The only ones on their toes after an accident...
are the tow trucks.
Drive like a wild man...and you may end up in a cage.
You can't charge traffic...without paying for it later.

Quips

Instead of trying to get ahead in traffic...
*   please use the one you already have.*

If you drive like lightning...you might crash like thunder.

The road might be rocky...if you drive when you're stoned.

Monkey around in traffic...and you may end up in a cage.

Some drivers get in the doghouse...
*   because they take too many nips.*

Drive like a musician...C Sharp or B Flat.

Those who have one for the road...
*   may have a policeman for a chaser.*

You'll never find that bluebird of happiness...
*   with too many swallows.*

Flying through traffic...is for the birds.

Undertakers can tell you...an accident is a grave situation.

Driving is like ordering a steak...
*   when you get home, be able to say well done.*

Those who like to live it up...may have to live it down.

If more people drive right...there will be more people left.

Having an accident is not the way to end the day...
*   as a smashing success.*

You'll never get to heaven...if you drive like the devil.

You may get grounded...if you drive when you're high.

Safety First...will make you last.

A heavy foot...is a step away from jail.

A drinking driver is like a gun...
*   both are dangerous when loaded.*

You'll never get burned...if your driving is matchless.

Getting your wires crossed in traffic...
    could be a shocking experience.
Driving with a heavy foot...is not the way to get your kicks.
Half the trouble in traffic...is caused by a fifth.
People who weave in and out of traffic...
    often end up in stitches.
Drivers who pass on hills...sometimes don't make the grade.
You won't have a ghost of a chance...
    if you drink too many spirits.
Driving when you're half high...
    is not the way to get up in the world.
The highway is not a racetrack...so any horseplay is a bad bet.
Pressing your luck in traffic...is not the way to iron things out.
You may be at the end of your rope...if you tie one on.
The amount of collisions caused by drinking drivers...
    is staggering.
Drive like a happy doctor...have a lot of patience.
The driver who thinks he's king of the road...may get crowned.
Drivers that have close shaves...often get clipped.
Never get bent out of shape...keep your driving straight.
When your driving is appealing...you're the top banana.
Drivers that use their noodle...never get into hot water.
Mind your driving manners...
    because you never know who you might run into.
Only morticians...dig accidents.
If you drive to beat the band...you may end up playing a harp.
Drivers with an axe to grind...often fly off the handle.

Quips

Drivers that play leapfrog in traffic...often croak.

You won't have a ghost of a chance...
if you don't have the right spirit

What's at stake is prime...and that's not a bum steer.

The way to avoid bouncing into someone else...
is to stay on the ball.

The reason we hammer at safety...
is to keep you from getting nailed.

If you try to pull something in traffic...
you may be stretching your luck.

Trying to shoot through traffic...may bang up your car.

If you have a hot time in the old town tonight...
you may end up in the cooler.

When you bank on safety...it's a lifetime saving.

Careless driving is like borrowing money...
it's always touch and go.

Get the best mileage home...by not driving half tanked.

When you stumble your way through traffic...
it's always a bad step.

Too many bottles...could become a case in court.

You'll never develop a nose for safety...
if you drive with a snoot full.

Motorists that drive too hard...often get arrest.

Be a joker in traffic...and you may get decked.

Dents on your car...make a bad impression.

Avoid bottling up traffic...by not driving half corked.

Things can really explode...if you drive when you're bombed.

If your wife wants to drive...don't stand in her way.

161

Motorists that drive too hard…often get arrest.
Be a joker in traffic…and you may get decked.
Dents on your car…make a bad impression.
Avoid bottling up traffic…by not driving half corked.
Things can really explode…if you drive when you're bombed.
If your wife wants to drive…don't stand in her way.
Drivers that keep in the groove…are never in a rut.
Acting like a comedian…
could become a smashing performance.
Safe drivers get the cheers…by avoiding the booze.
A sleepy driver…can become a wake.
You won't be taken to the cleaners…if your driving is spotless.
Tearing up the highway…could be the end of the road.
The trip home will be heavenly…if you drive like an angel.
Those who drive like the wind…may blow it.
Drinking and driving…is an arresting situation.
The road to court is not a freeway…it is expensive.
Always keep your train of thought…on the right track.
Trying to paint the town red tonight…
may give you the blues tomorrow.
That fine wine that improves with age…
is only sour grapes in traffic.
Too much booze… can give you the blues.
You may be carving your tombstone…if you chisel in traffic.
Those who drive when they're fractured…never get the breaks.
When you don't rub people the wrong way…
It's a much better feeling.

Quips

Drinking drivers are not very funny...
but they can still crack you up.

When highways are wet...the driver should stay dry.

The best part about being alcohol free...
is you never have to pay for it.

Don't shortchange yourself...by not driving with any sense.

That itching to get home quick...may be rash judgment.

Any time your driving looks fishy...
you may become the catch of the day.

Traffic is not going to be a circus...so keep your driving intense.

The best way to hold your liquor...is to keep it in the bottle.

Don't become a crank...by not getting too wound up.

A traffic ticket is not a lottery ticket...
you can't tear it up if you lose.

The only reason we nag at you...
is so you don't horse around in traffic.

Keep your driving well dressed...or it may become a lawsuit.

Try to pull the wool over a policeman's eyes...
and he may see through the yarn.

Safe driving will keep you out of the soup...
even when it's chilly.

If you horse around in traffic...
you may get saddled with a ticket.

Don't let your day go down the drain...
by forgetting today's safety plug.

When it's only coffee for the road...
there's always grounds for safety.

Don't let your day go down the drain…
by forgetting today's safety plug.

When it's only coffee for the road…
there's always grounds for safety.

Those who have too may glasses…
could become spectacles.

It's better to take a stand for safety…
than get a seat in court.

When there is so much rain…
there should not be a drip behind the wheel.

Alcohol may make you feel exhilarated…
but you may not be able to pronounce it.

You will not receive a rain check…
if you drive under the weather.

In wall-to-wall traffic…a driver cannot be half plastered.

Do not take common sense lightly…
because it carries a lot of weight.

If traffic seems like a jigsaw puzzle…
try to get home in one piece.

No one relishes…a pickled driver.

Safe driving in the rain…is never a dry run.

It takes a strong heart…to drive on clogged arteries.

A traffic jam…can be a sticky situation.

You cannot beat traffic…by whipping down the highway.

Aiming to get home safe…is something to shoot for.

You cannot be fit as a fiddle…if you get tight as a drum.

You may get sacked…if you drive half-in-the-bag.

Never be credited…with charging traffic.

Quips

Tipping the bottle…is one more downpour.

Try zipping up the highway…and you may get caught.

This message is not meant to bore you…only to drill it in you.

Never drive like an animal…when it's raining cats and dogs.

Staying away from the bottle…will keep you out of the jug.

Try to be a good egg…do not drive like you're half cracked.

Horsing around in traffic after dark…
    could become a nightmare.

Always drive with character…instead of acting like one.

Your day will stay bright… by not driving half lit.

The police will be busy as bees…
    trying to keep traffic buzzing along.

Keep your driving skills well polished…
    to avoid having a bad finish.

Anyone who's driving ability sparkles…is a real gem.

When it's a wet day…never let your driving get rusty.

Drinking drivers are like light bulbs…
    the first to get turned on are the first to burn out.

Safe driving is not being chicken…
    it's something to crow about.

Driving is like baseball…getting home safe is what counts.

Anyone who reaches for the bottle…
    may meet the long arm of the law.

Anyone who tries to bolt through traffic…is a real nut.

You always have the best time…when you keep a watch-out.

You cannot carry your own weight…
    if you drive when you're loaded.

Traffic court is like buying a car...it's hard to get a bargain.

If you drive like a turkey... you may be cooking your own goose.

We're giving you this pitch...so you don't strike out.

If you drive half in the bag...you may lose your grip.

Playing leapfrog in traffic...makes other drivers hopping mad.

Your temper can be an asset...so try not to lose it.

When the weather is for the ducks...
*   make sure you don't quack up.*

If you drive when you're stoned...you may hit rock bottom.

You cannot stay cool as a cucumber...
*   if you drive when you're pickled.*

Any animal behavior...is a pet peeve.

Trying to fly through traffic...is plain silly.

As you thread your way through traffic...
*   don't be on pins and needles.*

Too many cold ones...could put you on ice.

Are most of them silly and corny? Yes they are. I'll be the first to agree. But they worked for me, and if you use them, I hope they work for you!

Go Irish and Stay Safe!

-13-

Off the Beaten Path

NOTRE DAME FOOTBALL is all about traditions and for many fans there is tradition surrounding their entire weekend on campus. But sometimes tradition can turn into tedium. I mean how many times have you heard someone in the parking lot say "hey, where should we go to eat this weekend?"

You could go to the same old haunts or you could go to the same chain restaurant you have back home.

Or you could go where few of you have gone before. As a public service, direct from the Notre Dame Stadium press box, here is a list of local establishments that you may not know about but should get to know. All of them are very local, reasonably priced and somewhere up on the walls they display their loyalty to the Fighting Irish.

Skillet Restaurant

At the corner of Ironwood Drive and McKinley Avenue, The Skillet is now open to the public Friday, Saturday and Sunday and on all three days they serve a South Bend tradition, a Polish buffet. And it is all you can eat.

And some customers take that very seriously. Located just a few miles from campus, I highly recommend ordering their broasted chicken for your tailgate party. They will fix as much or as little as you want and have it ready to go in a container that will keep it warm for hours. The best in town. Oh, try their homemade pies too.

Blue Lantern

About 15 minutes from campus, this bar/restaurant has been a favorite in Mishawaka for decades. Very clean with a terrific staff and the owner will often meet you at the door.

Great seafood on the menu, especially the perch, cod and frog legs. The waitresses get to know their customers by name and make you feel like family. The chicken noodle soup is better than mom's.

Silver Tower Seafood House

The Silver Tower has been around at least since I came to Notre Dame and is something akin to a generational hand-me-down in South Bend. Yes, seafood is the specialty but the steaks are good too. Located on the near west side of South Bend where the folks are loyal to Notre Dame win or lose.

Hensell's Oaken Bucket

About 15 minutes from campus and just east of Indiana University South Bend. Great hamburgers and a nice variety of beer on tap. For games early in the season you can sit outside where the deck is next to the Saint Joseph River. A good place to go to get away from the crowd on Friday nights and the staff will take good care of you if you get there late after a game.

Louvered Door

Also on the west side of South Bend, it has been a favorite hangout for years for South Bend politicians and lawyers. Terrific sandwiches for lunch and full-service dinners at night. The staff is knowledgeable and friendly. They make a top of the line Bloody Mary too.

Cedar House Restaurant

Just five minutes from campus this might be the best breakfast in town. Maybe you think scrambled eggs are just scrambled eggs but I beg to differ. Omelets are a favorite of many customers. Has the feel of real diner because that is what it is, a diner. Lunch and dinner menus too. Very reasonably priced as a good diner should be.

Redemaks

A legend in New Buffalo, Michigan. Huge menu but you don't need one. Just order the double cheeseburger (Velveeta never tasted so good) and some fries and a milkshake.

If you are coming to Notre Dame from the Chicago area it is worth going a little out of your way coming or going home. They close for the winter at the end of October.

Red Arrow Roadhouse

I saved the best for last. This is my favorite restaurant in Michiana and well worth the trip from South Bend. It gets very crowded in the summer and the first part of football season but it is worth any wait you might have. The nightly specials are always interesting and diverse. Tim's chicken dinner is irresistible. You can get directions through their website but it is hard to miss when there is only one flashing traffic light in beautiful Union Pier, Michigan. If the weather is good make sure you save enough time for a quick drive to New Buffalo and a walk on the public beach. If you find yourself drained following the dinner and the walk, stop at Casey's Bar and Restaurant in downtown New Buffalo for refreshment.

Notre Dame Dining Halls
(South and North)

For some fans this is part of their weekend tradition. For many others, I am willing to bet they don't even know the halls are open to the general public. This is not your father's dining hall food. Notre Dame continues to take their student cuisine to new levels and you can enjoy it too. Brunch is available on both Saturday and Sunday and wait until you see the options.

And, are you ready for this—they have candlelight dinners after the game! The lines can get long but there is a way to shorten the wait. If you know a student at Notre Dame have them charge your meal in advance to their student card. If it is one of your children, remind them about the tuition you are paying and maybe they won't ask you to pay them back. Unlikely, of course, but even if you pay, take my word it is well worth it. Good food, great experience.

The Buffalo Rose Bistro and Pizzeria

If you are coming from or heading south on highway 31, a quaint, new spot is The Buffalo Rose Bistro and Pizzaria in Lakeville, 11 miles south of South Bend. It is located next to The Working Person's Store on 31. The Bistro has everything from Italian to barbecue to hand-tossed pizza and a full bar.

In pleasant weather you can eat outside. Good food, intimate, pleasant surroundings make this a destination that is convenient but away from the crowd.